Nowt's Same

It's your belly at keeps your back up; you can't work wi'out some packing.
Heard in Swaledale

You could get plenty o' work ... trouble was you didn't get enough brass for it.
Gurt Bill, Swaledale

If there was a shilling to be made, forty men went after it.
Said of Greenhow Hill, in the late 1920s.

There nivver were any "good owd days." They're far better now.
A Nidderdale farmer, c1950.

It's come to summat when they've putten lasses into pants.
Wensleydale man, beholding a group of Land Girls

Once the hill farmers started to wed lasses from "away," they married trouble.
Overhead at Hawes Auction Mart.

People think of the Women's Institute members as all tweeds, twin-sets and pearls. We just omitted the tweeds and twin-sets.
A member of Rylstone WI at the launch of a charity calendar featuring pictures of the ladies in their birthday-suits, 1999.

... James Herriot wrote from the heart about the Dales as he knew them, a countryside and a way of life which is being swept away by tourism, incomers and the various lunacies of the National Parks.
Malcolm Barker, in a book review, Yorkshire Post, April 22, 1999.

Nowt's Same

A light-hearted review of Dales life in the 20th century

by W R Mitchell

Illustrations by Richard Bancroft

CASTLEBERG
1999

Contents

Cover Illustrations
Front – Turning swathes, Wensleydale. Jack Foster, butcher and fiddler of Austwick. A modern quad or all-terrain vehicle. Sledge-boy, with a load of loose hay, Wensleydale. A shepherd near Clapham. Farmer at the head of Walden.
Back – The Coultherd family of Clapham. Scotch hands, butter bowl and butter stamp, all made of sycamore. A Northern Dairy Shorthorn. Dalesman at the head of Coverdale. Washing the sheep before clipping, Keasden.

Ther's motor charas, cars, an' bikes, noo,
fleein' iverywhaur,
We've noo an' than an aeroplane – i' peace
As weel as war;
Ther's gramaphones 'at play an' sing – they keep
some fooak alive,
An' yan wonders if ther'll be owt fresh
I' twenty-twenty-five.

John Thwaite, a Wensleydale poet

A **Castleberg** Book.
First published in the United Kingdom in 1999.
Text, © W R Mitchell 1999.
The moral right of the author has been asserted.
ISBN 1 871064 66 X
Typeset in Palatino, printed and bound in the United Kingdom by Lamberts Print & Design, Station Road, Settle, North Yorkshire, BD24 9AA.
Published by Castleberg, 18 Yealand Avenue, Giggleswick, Settle, North Yorkshire, BD24 0AY.

Foreword

by

Fred Trueman, OBE

A s ONE Millennium draws to a close, many of us will be looking back on events in the 20th century. Amusing tales are like "memory hooks," reminding us of events in our lives.

One tale that helps me to recall my cricketing days is of the Nidderdale man who turned up early for a match at Headingley, intending also to renew his subscription to the Yorkshire Cricket Club.

While chatting with the secretary, the low attendance at the match was mentioned. The dalesman said: "There'll be a lot more this afternoon." When asked how he knew this, he said: "It's half day closing in Pateley Bridge."

There are many such tales in this entertaining book.

Introduction

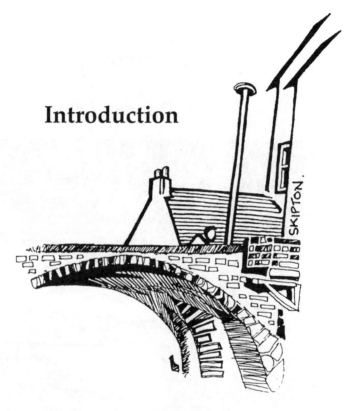

I WAS BORN in Skipton, "gateway to the Yorkshire Dales," at a time when a forest of mill chimneys breathed black smoke into the Pennine air and crows flew backwards to keep the grit out of their eyes. To the south lay yet more industry, but go north – through the "gateway" – and you entered the dale-country. Here were alternating valleys and ridges, with packy clouds and soot-free sheep, becks you might paddle in, rivers stocked with brown trout and purple-headed hills resounding to the gruff voices of grouse.

King Cotton, who sneaked into westernmost Yorkshire from Lancashire via the Aire Gap, annexed Skipton but did not snuff out the pre-industrial flavour of a town named after its ancient pre-occupation with sheep. Historical connections were cherished. I grew up believing that Anne Clifford was one of my aunts. Mother talked about her as she wheeled me in a push-chair beside the castle gateway and up the Bailey. Auntie Anne was in fact *Lady* Anne Clifford, last of an illustrious family to bear the Clifford name. And she'd died in 1676.

You could see her monogram on a window in the parish church, where I was baptised (I was later hi-jacked by the Methodists). The Clifford family motto, *Des or Mais*, was fixed for all time in letters of stone above that splendid castle gateway, flanked by drum-towers. That small boy (me) would eventually meet a descendant, Lord Hothfield, in one of the grand rooms of Appleby castle where, after looking at a celebrated triptych featuring Lady Anne he described her as "quite a gel."

As a market town, Skipton served the Craven Dales and periodically the High Street filled with dalesfolk, mostly farmers, wearing cloth caps, their best tweedy setting-off suits, well polished gaiters and (ditto) boots. Years before, when a horse and trap were owned by the better-end of the farming community, the traps had been tipped up in rows and the horses given temporary quarters and a good helping of oats or bran in stables behind local inns.

Market-fresh farmers (i.e., those who liked to drink something stronger than lemonade) relied on their horses to get them home. While one man was making yet another call at a roadside tavern, local lads had taken the horse out of the shafts and put it back facing the wrong way. The bemused farmer left the inn, blinked several times and remarked: "I'd nivver have thought a hoss could throw a cart ower its head."

Mr Ward, the blacksmith at a smithy near Mill Bridge, was approached by a farmer who had a hair lodged beside an eye. The smith, offering him the anvil as a seat, deftly removed the hair, then (knowing the farmer had a mean streak) said: "Is ta bahn to tak t'hair wi' thee – or pick it up on thi way home?" Haggling over the sale or purchase of a cow was protracted. A farmer's lile lad, tired of waiting for the handclasp that sealed a bargain, gave a deep sigh and said to his father: "Get the begger selled."

After years during which cattle brought for sale had stood in the

High Street, the cause of hygiene triumphed. An auction mart was established within moo-ing or bleating distance of the Midland's railway station. The horse fair was held during my early years and I remember when the July Barbers arrived. These were Irishmen from County Mayo, keen to help with the hay harvest for a month at a time. They were paid little but had their "keep." If the weather was wet, they whitewashed the outbuildings, a process known as "bug-blinding."

When cattle for sale stood in the High Street, the farmers needed to wear their heavy-duty galluses [braces] to hold up their trousers, such was the weight of sovereigns in their pockets. I remember one farmer with means who had the irritating habit of jingling coins in his pocket as he spoke. What was the point of having "brass" if nobody knew about it? When I asked a certain West Craven farmer how he was, he replied: "Aw reet," hastily qualifying this with the words "in health."

A self-respecting farmer bought his suits at Breares in Middle Row and was still wearing them up thirty years later. The farmer's wife bought her corsets from Miss Cairns and her dresses from Mrs Ambler. Everything would be taken "on appro" and if there were second thoughts about anything it would be returned the next day.

Hardworking millfolk formed the base of a social pyramid dominated by Lord Hothfield and his friends, senior clergy, doctors and solicitors. Milltown consisted of terraced houses, ginnel 'oles and snickets. Almost every utterance seemed to begin with the words "Na think on..." Almost every house had a strap, or piece of leather, from the mill, hanging by the fireside. This was the Great Deterrent. A wayward child would be "leathered" or "belted." In the days before a National Health Service, doctors cost money and home remedies were invariably used.

A sore throat was eased by being poulticed and for a chest complaint there was a ritual of spreading goose grease (saved from the bird eaten last Christmas) on brown paper and stuck on to the inside of the juvenile's vest with safety pins just before bedtime. The brown paper crackled until it had softened. A child with whooping cough was made to stand in the fumes rising from where roadmen were spraying tar on the road prior to giving it a coating of stone chippings.

When the 20th century dawned, most Skipton families provided inexpensive labour for Dewhurst's Mill and the other textile enterprises. Several times a day, t'mill buzzer roared out like a peevish bull, controlling the flow and ebb of a drab army – the grey mass of workers whose homes were mainly in Middle Town, its terraced houses forming a grid-iron pattern on what had been pleasant green hillocks.

Houses of modest size were given splendid names. The Anne Clifford connection led to the naming of Sackville Street, Dorset Street and Brougham Street, the favourite of her several castles standing at Brougham, near Penrith. Anne would have sniffed with derision could she have known that another street would be named after a man who, to her, was the hateful Cromwell.

Skipton was virtually ringed by moors. At times, the breeze brought down a whiff of peat. Then, with a change of wind, whole areas would be blotted out by acrid smoke from a forest of mill chimneys. Anyone with chest problems wheezed. The sparrows developed a dry cough. A cyclist, leaving town for a run in the Dales, asked about "the funny smell" and was told: "It's fresh air, lad." The steady deposition of soot from mill  chimneys did ensure that the roses in tiny front gardens were free of "black spot" and other fungal complaints. The housewives of Skipton waged war against grime with hot water, carbolic soap and donkeystones. Heaven help anyone who walked on a newly-swilled stretch of pavement.

11

Springtime came to Middletown with the flowering of dandelions, the only plants with the vigour to grow widely in an area blotted out by bricks, mortar, paving flags and stone setts. A clump of mint in a bucket of jaded soil stood near one of the back doors and provided the means for making mint sauce when the lady of the house had chosen mutton for the week-end joint.

Mum, born in 1900, scrimped and saved her way through two world wars and an industrial slump. When she was carrying me, she was operating several looms at a local mill. I was born in 1928, when the textile trade was slack, mill chimneys were smokeless, mill cats were lean and the staple food for many families was bread and dripping. One despairing mother gave a child a piece of bread and told her to run round to her auntie and ask her to put some butter on it.

Early in life, I developed a passion for history, or what one of our Dales friends called, somewhat derisively, "t'long-deeard past." That interest had begun, perhaps, with an exploration of Gran's house, which stood a few doors away from our own. If the weather was inclement on a Sunday, the family photograph album was brought out and the pictures of poker-faced relatives, grouped in t'front street or outside Morecambe boarding houses during a brief summer holiday, were laughed over.

Gran's house had a large attic that, to me, was as still and mysterious as an Egyptian tomb, being half full of faded treasures, longer used, though Gran – in typical Yorkshire fashion - thought they "might come in one day." Here was an old chair (broken), a stuffed owl (sun-bleached), a pile of receipts (yellowing), a tickless clock, a framed photograph of – who-knows-who? A purple vase had been a wedding gift from an aunt. The vase was washed and displayed only when a visit from her was expected.

Now and again I was allowed to enter Gran's front room or parlour. It was unused except at Christmas or when "comp'ny" was expected or when, once a week, Gran attended to the family aspidistra, anointing its fleshy leaves with cold tea. At Gran's house, unchanged since it was built in Victoria's heyday, stone steps led down into a flagged cellar where stood implements of torture, used on Monday, which was wash-day. The mangle had an iron frame and wooden rollers that crushed the finger-ends of the unwary. A galvanised dolly-tub and a fluted board sufficed in the days before washing machines.

Hanging from a wall in the backyard at Gran's house was a zinc bath, which was trundled noisily indoors on Friday evenings, when each member of the family, the youngest first, went through a ritualised bathing routine before a cheery coal fire. A visitor who felt embarrassed when an attractive young lady began to undress prior to having a bath was told by her father not to worry. "She's a careful lass; she won't splash you."

Most houses lacked central heating. I awoke in winter to see frost-patterns on the window and I shuddered when my warm feet encountered cold linoleum. The lamp-lighter went on his evening rounds, using his long rod to switch on and ignite the gas lamps. Today, the town is bathed in the orange glare of sodium chloride under which people look sickly and red cars appear to be painted cream.

The High Street – this "gateway to the Dales" – has lost many of its family firms but market day stalls still appear like mushrooms in a damp meadow. Shoppers and day-trippers shuffle along crowded pavements. And the ghost of Lady Anne Clifford still haunts the church and castle where she was so much at home.

Anne Clifford

1900-1909

This was a decade when almost every job was done by hand by a large reserve of inexpensive labour, hired for next-to-nothing on a half-yearly basis. As one man said: "You were either working or you were in bed, fast asleep." Some social ladder-climbing was possible, such as when a lass, hired as a servant, married the farmer's son. It was a period when bread was home-baked, oatmeal was a staple food and you might buy a pound of butter for sixpence.

Up t'Dales

IN THE upper dale-country, the valleys narrow and become rockier. Becks gush down brant [steep] hillsides to give the rivers a transfusion of cold water. Norman Swindlehurst, reared at a moor-edge farm, described the land as "curlew country," adding: "It's upland, with white bent [a coarse grass] and rushes. We had to make the best of what we had." His neighbour spoke of the geology as "that queer in-between stuff...Some of t'stone doesn't knaw if it's limestone or sandstone."

At the dalehead, summer was a short intermission between two long winters. In an upland valley like Walden, a tributary of Wensleydale, the sheep and lambs had to be kept in the meadows until well into May. With land fed simply on "muck," a farmer did not expect to see a proper flush of grass till t'end o' June "and it gives up growing in August."

Hereabouts, in a landscape of low horizons, of peat, heather, sphagnum moss and bog, "the lean lands rake the sky." I am quoting Halliwell Sutcliffe, novelist and "man of the moors," who loved them at any season but especially in late summer, when the flowering of heather gives the impression a giant has laid a purple carpet across the tops.

Many a dalesman was as heafed to a moorland situation as his sheep, which had drunk in a love of the area with their mother's milk. A dalesman who decided to tear himself away from his natal area had his resolve weakened when a cock grouse shouted: *kowa, kowa*. As it sounded just like *go back, go back*, he turned and went back home. Subsequently, a visitor asked him what he did in such a bleak setting in winter. The farmer replied: "Same as in summer – but wi' me overcoat on!"

When a new century dawned, the moorlands were under the control of gamekeepers. Hardly anyone else ventured on to them. Even the farmer needed the keeper's permission to attend to his moor-going sheep. Permission was not likely to be granted if it was a sensitive time in the life-cycle of grouse. An exception was the poacher, who arrived surreptitiously by night.

The Weardale Gang were brazen. They stormed the Swaledale moors at any time, bagging what they could, and sometimes peevishly setting fire to the moor if the pickings were poor. Grouse-shooting put a bit o' brass in the pockets of local people. A farmer would hire a horse that was used to transport food to the shooting lodge. Other horses were available to convey women to the butts.

The hut used for refreshments was a two-roomed affair, with one room for the gentry and the other for the beaters. The gentry had a hamper filled with goodies and washed them down with good wine. The beaters had to "mash" some tea and eat beef sandwiches. "One year, they forgot to send up some bread. We still had our sandwiches – a bit o' fat 'tween a couple o' pieces o' lean meat."

Dales weather is transient. At its worst, it inspired an old chap to say: "I reckon this morning looks as if it was up aw neet." In Swaledale, where the weather has always been taken seriously, conditions were not just hot or cold, wet or dry. It might be *brimmin* [misty after a thaw of snow], *clashy* [wet and windy] or *glave* [cold, shivery]. If the sun was too bright, too early in the day, it was *glisky* or *glishy*. One shouldn't expect the good conditions to last. In summer it was *gussy* [growy] and in winter *himey* [layered with hoar frost]. A day when big white clouds sailed across the azure blue like galleons under full sail was *packy*.

Winter began with the weather *tewtlin*. A few flakes of snow would be seen dancing in the air. Then it was *stourin*. A wind had sprung up.

The snowfall intensified. When it was raw in winter it was *snizy*. Came the thaw. It was *brimmin* once again. The postman donned his clogs and on his morning round they were turning *t'snaw broth* [melting snow].

It might be raining on one side of the dale and sunny on the other. At haytime, when a minor whirlwind carried wisps of hay aloft, the farmer forecast that another wet spell was on the way. The same forecast would apply if the wind had not whirled. Dales farming is ruled by the weather and the seasons rather than by t'clock. When Summer Time was introduced, an old chap said: "Up here, pushin' clocks forrards and back'ards doesn't mak much difference. T'weather'll suit itsen."

Life on the upland farms was hard and the financial rewards meagre. One who was reared in Upper Wharfedale said: "We were browt up on oatmeal and mouse droppings." Photographs taken by a Mr Brundritt of Bradford in 1900 provided an insight into the lives of George and Jane Beresford, who moved from Thorpe to Cowside in Langstrothdale in 1896 and, by the turn of the century, had a large and still growing family. On one photograph, George is seen wearing a back-can by which milk was conveyed from cows milked at the outbarns to the house.

Hygiene in milk production was not regarded as a major concern. A Dentdale farmer said: "Milk tastes o' nowt till t'cow's had its foot in t'bucket." Milking was by hand, of course, with the farmer sitting on the traditional three-legged stool, cap turned so the neb was at the back, legs clamped on either side of a bucket into which he coaxed milk from laden teats. The dominant sound was that of milk spurting against metal.

A Dentdale farmer urged his man to milk briskly, so foam was produced to carry over the rim of the pail any stray bits o' muck. The milker tried to do something to stop the cows swishing its tail for if it drew it across the face of the milker, he might be injured by one of the hard bits of dung caught in the hair and known as a "muck-button."

On another photograph taken by Mr Brundritt, the farmer, George Beresford, is seen holding the reins of a horse harnessed to a trap in which his wife and family have settled themselves, in joyful anticipation of a trip to market. Horses did the heavy jobs on the land. A man who bought a horse returned it – as he was permitted to do – because he had detected a fault. The seller was told: "Yon hoss won't hold its head up." The reply was: "It's a proud hoss. Thee get it paid for!"

The photograph of Jane shows a round-faced woman, plain as a pikestaff, with a long, stiffly-laundered white pinafore. She would have a hectic life. The living room was always crowded because her husband kept the provender for his stock there. It was drier than in the out-buildings. When another child was due, a message was sent to Mrs Roland Parker, of Deepdale, who acted as midwife, though she had no formal qualifications. Someone rode over Fleet Moss to tell the Hawes doctor of the impending birth, which had usually taken place when he arrived. It was said of one Dales medical practitioner that by the time he arrived the child was almost ready for school.

George Beresford died of appendicitis; he passed away quickly, with-out fuss, in April, 1905, aged 48. His body was taken by horse-drawn hearse along the dale road, to a last resting-place among his ancestors in the yard of Hubberholme church. Jane left the farm at the back-end of that year. Dalesfolk were facing lean times. Wool fetched a miserable $2^1/_2$d a pound.

As a new century opened, characters abounded. There were lots of people who'd nivver strayed away from their native valley. One of them, who lived in upper Swaledale, told me: "It's not so bad as long as thou isn't snowed up I' bed." His farm was on the hillside, facing north-east, from whence cometh the snow that sticks. He'd retired to bed, as usual, with his window half open, to admit some of God's fresh air. During the night, a blizzard – "such a whizziker" – drove snow into the bedroom. He awoke to find a film of snow on everything "'cept t'place where I were liggin. That spot had thawed out."

By a happy chance, I usually arrived at his house on baking day. There was his wife, with flour up to her elbows and the house flavoured with the homely smell of fresh scones or cake. He had the picturesque speech of one born, reared and resident in the Dales. He "telled" me about three lasses, the daughters of a local family, two of whom were now dead. As he put it: "There's nobbut yan on 'em wick now."

He mentioned Tommy Metcalfe, who went from Swaledale to Wensleydale ower t'Buttertubs, with a hoss and flat cart. The dalesfolk knew it as the Midnight Express, which was ironical. "T'oss was so slow you couldn't tell whether he was stopped or going." Dusk was "t'edge o' dark." If this dalesman was feeling wonderfully fit, he was "as peeart as a lop [hare]" and if he had not been able to get into a working rhythm he had "not struck a bat."

James Norman Swindlehurst, who was nobbut a lad at a lile farm up Keasden when the 20th century opened, had moved with his family from Barrow-in-Furness when his father, who had worked for t'Quarp [Co-op] was advised by his doctor to get an outdoor job. The choice was Brackengarth, which was owned by a member of the family. This was one of a string of little farms extending up the moorside from Clapham to Bowland Knotts.

A horse and cart moved all their possessions, with an overnight stop at the home of relatives in Kirkby Lonsdale. When the last load was being moved up the hill, with the children hanging on grimly, one of the Swindlehurst lasses pointed through the gloom to a building on the skyline. She asked her mother if this was where they would keep the cows. "No, love," said mother. "That's where we're going to live."

Brackengarth, about forty acres in extent, was open to all the winds that blew but with some bonnie views, including the Three Peaks of Whernside, Ingleborough and Penyghent. The ground floor was slate-flagged. Mother scrubbed the blue flags till they shone. You could tell when it was going to rain, for then the slate "came up damp." The ever-busy Mother bought salt in a huge block and attacked it with a knife, after which she pulverised the bits with a rolling pin.

There was a nightly ritual of trimming the lamp-wicks. When the chimney was to be cleaned, a holly bush was tied to a cart rope and lowered into the gloomy void before being jerked up and down to displace the soot. In the absence of taps, water was transported from a beck with "ladin" can and bucket. When it was time for the walls to be lime-washed, someone took a horse and cart to the quarry at Giggleswick and brought back some cob-lime. This had to be "slacked" in water before it could be used. During a wet haytime, helpers were given the gainful task of lime-washing the insides of the shippons.

A ham from the slaughtered pig was left hanging for a year to improve the flavour. As Norman told me: "People don't give pork time to cure today. They're eating it almost before the pig's dead." His lively memory included collecting coal from the pit at Ingleton, the cost being sixpence a hundredweight. "You backed under a chute; a man pulled a lever and *shoooo* – down came the coal. You had to fair stick to your horse or it would have bolted...A chap who sold coal at Clapham station was so precise it weighing it out he kept a row of assorted cobs of coal so that the customer received the precise amount he had ordered."

The Swindlehursts were typical of a race of small-time farmers. They had enormous self-reliance and strength of spirit. They gloried in their independence. They bent rather than broke in the face of adversity. They had a native wit. Two friends met after several years. One said: "I thought thou were deeard." The reply was: "So I am. I'm too lazy to stiffen."

In the unchanging days before the eruption of the Great War in 1914, the Dales farming year ran an unvarying and periodically busy course. The highspots were tupping, lambing, cutting t'peearts, clipping t'sheep, haytime, rush-gathering for bedding young stock, and pig-killing. A typical upland farmer "selled a bit o' milk, a bit o'butter and a few eggs." Then he had to wait for his surplus sheep to mak some brass at t'back-end.

There was a neighbourliness in the Dales. If there was an operation like sheep-washing and clipping, it was undertaken communally, taking each farm in rotation. Large familes were reared. One of the host of Metcalfes added to the complexity of family relationships by having 19 kids. Five or six kids in a family was nowt unusual. One family consisted of 20 children – twice. The explanation was that one died, making 19, and the couple had yet another, bringing it back up to 20.

The Dales farmer was primarily a sheep man. He knew every animal in his flock. A farm labourer said: "My boss would stand and watch and smoke his pipe and say of one animal: 'She'll lamb afore mornin'. And she did! He really watched his sheep – how they walked, what they did. He'd get up at night and go out with a lantern. He lived with yon sheep, day and neet, through lambing time."

Norman Swindlehurst went as far as Kirkby Stephen for a good tup and brought it back by rail and road. He would explain: "It was rail to Settle, road between Settle and Giggleswick stations, rail to Clapham, then road up the hill to the farm. By the time I got home I was tired. So was t'tup." When a livestock fair was held in the street at Clapham towards the end of September, farmers took hurdles and "med bits o' pens against folks's doors. Them folks were 'fast' in their houses."

An old woman called Moore, from Crooklands, who was a bit mannish, attended Clapham fair. "She had to be mannish, t'questions she asked t'menfolk. It suited me when I was a lad. She'd examine a tup and ask: 'And what sort of a gitter is he?' I thought it was cobbed [droll] that a woman should be asking such questions."

Better End o' t'Poor

WITH POVERTY endemic, you might be "short o' brass" or "baht," in which case you "hadn't a penny to scratch your bottom with." A wealthy dalesman was said to be "bow-legged wi' brass."

"Makkin' ends meet" was a continuing problem in the Dales. In lean times, the farmers went into a state of semi-hibernation. There was never "brass to throw about." If it was thrown, then you'd hear it, for the gold sovereign was in use. If anyone bought a beeast, then one or two sovereigns were exchanged. The buyer expected "a bit o' luck," 'appen a bob [shilling].

The tale was told of a farmer and his wife who arrived at the bank with a pocket full of sovereigns and asked the cashier to count it while they were there. It could then be added to their account. The cashier did so and announced a figure – say, 1,768. A recount was demanded. The result was the same. Said the farmer to his wife: "We browt t'wrong bucket!"

For a time, paper money was distrusted. In truly hard times no farmer hung on to a cheque he received. One who started selling milk to a dairy at Bainbridge discovered the owner was on the verge of bankruptcy. Whenever a cheque came in for the month's milk, he sent one of his family rushing up to the bank – and he prayed that the cheque wouldn't bounce back!

When Mr Hird of Yockenthwaite had some good lambs to sell, he was visited by a dealer, Mr Wrathall of Skipton, who agreed to buy them and made out a cheque for the full amount. They arranged to have the lambs driven to a point lower down the dale the following morning. Here a drover appointed by Mr Wrathall would collect them.

The drover set off up Wharfedale, passing on the way a farmer on a white horse travelling at speed towards Skipton. The lambs were not in the appointed place and so the drover continued to walk up to Yockenthwaite, where he saw the lambs in a field close to the farm. It seems that Mr Hird had been uneasy about having been paid by cheque. He asked his brother to go to the bank at Skipton to have it cleared. This the brother did, using a white horse.

When the brother returned, with the news that the cheque was in order, the lambs were released and the drover was provided with a good meal before leaving Yockenthwaite for Skipton. In the following year, Mr Wrathall avoided all the fuss by paying for lambs with guineas taken from a large bag.

One answer to limited funds was to adopt the barter system. Instead of buying a cockerel from someone for 5s, you'd bargain, then take a couple o' pullets in exchange. In the years before the 1914-18 war, a quarryman at Burtersett was paid 18s a week – 16s.2d after deductions. He kept a few hens and a few geese. The income from these covered the cost of "extras", like new clothing for the kids.

In Dentdale, a lass who in the early 1900s got a job helping in a farm-house worked a twelve hour day for a shilling. Her father, a quarryman, "walked up t'dale and reet out on t'top of t'fell, where a slate quarry had been oppened up. He worked a day, walked back home – and was paid half a crown. A rheumaticky man who walked from Hardraw to Burtersett quarry each weekday arrived at work when it commenced at 7-30, was never late, gave a lifetime of service to the quarry – and never earned more than 16s a week.

Jack Tate, who shepherded on Walden Moor and Bishopdale Moor for many years, eventually became a nomad in the dale, patronising pubs and sleeping in barns. He helped farmers at haytime. When he was paid for this work, he bought himself a pair of good shoes and trousers. On running out of tobacco, he smoked leaves.

A farmer found Jack "liggin" in the barn at High Fors. It was the first day of May and all was white with frost. He had "near starved to deeath," because there was not enough hay left to give him sufficient cover. When the farmer's wife gave him a bit o' breakfast, he said: "By gow, that was t'best meal I've had for a lang while. Can you lend us a bob?"

Mills is Mucky

IF YOU'RE apt to think of the Yorkshire Dales as a green and pleasant landscape, think again. This area has been highly industrialised. And mills is mucky. The water-powered mills were acceptable but when it came to mills with chimneys nearly everyone developed a dry cough.

Mills where lead was smelted were the worst. A good draught was required, so they ran a flue across the moor to some high point, where they stuck the chimney. This belched smoke and fumes that killed off the vegetation round about and gave the moorland sheep a slighter darker hue. Meanwhile, anyone who would was given a brush and told to clean out the flues to recover the last bit of lead. Such a worker was not a good insurance risk.

King Cotton reigned at Skipton, Airton, Langcliffe, Linton and many other places up t'Dales, where the mill-owners imported coal and cheap labour, including child labour from as far away as Cornwall. At Langcliffe, a buzzer heralded the start of the working day, giving workers just enough time to done shawls and clogs as well as their workaday wear and go clatteringly down a lonnin [lane] to where the machines awaited them.

It was a custom in town to impose a penny fine on any worker who reported late. A man who was habitually late was met by the master, who asked: "Do you know what time we start work?" Said the laggard worker: "No. They've allus started by t'time I get here." The maister said, testily, to another late-comer: "The buzzer's gone." The worker replied: "They'll pinch owt these days."

At Skipton, with every change of wind, the smoke which theoretically rose above the town to form its own black cloud would be wafted along the streets, ensuring the rose bushes in front gardens would not get black-spot by covering everything with a veneer of soot.

When mother left school, at the age of 14, she got weaving in a literal sense, entering a world of damp cotton and chattering looms. There was a daily flow and ebb of workers twixt their homes and the mills. At an unearthy hour, the textile army was on the move. Stone pavements resounded with the clattering to iron-shod clogs. A stranger who awoke to such a clatter thought a troop of cavalry was passing through the town. Shawls and clogs were the distinctive wear of the older weavers.

In becoming a weaver, Mother did the accepted thing. Most of the young ladies leaving school went millwards. A weaver married, settling in a little terrace house in Middletown or Newtown, up Gargrave Road or down Broughton Road. She bore children, scoured and donkey-stoned the front doorstep as a sign of respectabiltity, grew old – then died.

Meanwhile, the mucky mills belched forth black smoke. As it swept down the streets, it was so thick you could taste it.

Summat to Eat

A N OLD-TIME Dales kitchen was flagged and, periodically, the flags were strewn with a hard sand kept in a barrel. During a wet haytime, if a senior member of the family saw that the Irishmen had nothing to do, they would say: "Thou mun bray sand today." This consisted of pulverising blocks of sandstone with big hammers.

The kitchen walls were lime-washed, mainly white, but some pink. The slopstone [kitchen sink] was made of a large piece of stone, more rarely slate. If there was a tap it delivered cold water, the hot water being drawn from a boiler beside the fireplace which rose in cast iron splendour almost to the ceiling. On the opposite side of the fire was an oven.

Work was carried out on a deal-top table which was flanked by forms with a robust chair at either end. Grandfather sat at the head of the table. All self-respecting women made bread at home. Housewives who bought bread were considered to be "shiftless." There was one big baking day each week. The family almost lived on bread.

It's your stomach that 'ods your back up. Porridge was a staple food in most Dales homes. It must have some body about it – enough to ensure that, as in the Lake District, a mouse might walk dryshod across it. To oatmeal porridge was added plenty of black treacle, which cost a penny a jar.

Blue [skimmed] milk was used on porridge. At one farm, porridge was made in a big pan, which had a handle that allowed it to be suspended from a reckon, over an open fire. Blue milk was poured into the pan and when it was nearly on the boil, oatmeal was added. If you poured it too fast, lumps were formed and these were called dog-'eeards. If you had a fall of soot, you had sooty porridge.

In Craven, porridge was made in a brass pan over the kitchen fire, the porridge being stirred with a wooden stick known as a thible. How thick was the porridge depended on personal preferences. One man liked it so stiff that it was handled to him in a basin, which he turned over. The basin was removed. The porridge resembled blancmange and was shiny on top. The diner put a hole in the middle and poured into it a spoonful of syrup. Blue milk formed a sort of moat.

Two other oaten products were haverbread (round and "a bit shaggy at t'edges) and oatcake (resembling a wash-leather, especially when it was hung up to dry on a rack suspended from the kitchen ceiling). The type of bowl popular for oatcake making was that made at Black Burton [Burton-in-Lonsdale] which were brown outside and yellow within. Oatmeal was emptied into the bowl. There followed fat, the mixture being kneaded, as with bread.

The oakcake was cooked on a flat, heated surface known as a back-stone, which had to be well greased with bacon fat. Some of the mixture was taken from the bowl, and a pinch of bicarbonate of soda was added. If times were bad, it was bread and dripping or, as one despairing

farmer called it, "bread and spit." Clara Sedgwick told me: "We had three days of baking haverbread for haytime. There was nothing better than this, especially if there was plenty of home-made butter on it and a right good pot o' coffee to help wash it down."

A Littondale man who had some town lads helping him with hay-time gave them rabbit at every meal. At the end of the week he said: "Well, lads, I suppose you're ready for your rabbit pie." Said one lad, wearily: "What I want is a bloody ferret."

Flour arrived at a farm in a 10-stone bag. The bowl used for baking held two stones of flour. The maker of bread used half a pound of yeast, a great big handful of salt and mixed them with milk and water before letting the mixture stand on the hearth. It was enough to make twelve loaves and perhaps a cob [small, round loaf] as well.

Brown bread was uncommon. At one farm the type made was "coarse bread." The daughter went down into the foddergang [in the barn] where the rows of cattle provender were found. She took a basin and half-filled it with bran, mixing it in with the plain white dough. It made a beautiful "brown" bread. For soda bread, you used soda instead of yeast. It was best eaten on the day it was made, for it soon went hard. Eggs were preserved in a "water glass." The accent was on economy in the house. Folk lived as cheaply as possible; it was not a mark of poverty but just sensible house-keeping.

The special food at Christmas was goose, plum pudding or barley pudding (made of barley, with the addition of currants and raisins and a right good sauce wi' either some rum or whisky in it). When the geese had been killed, giblet pie could be made of meat from the neck and gizzard; plus the heart; it was boiled and served in a dish with a crust on.

Clean and Decent

A T COAT FAW, a big farm beyond Dent Town, the farmhouse was big. "You could have driven a horse and cart through t'front door and down t'passage." On the ground floor was a living room and a front room, also a big cellar with stone slabs where we put the butter we made. It kept rock-hard, even in summer. There were seven bedrooms on the first floor and up above were two attic rooms. It was said the place was first intended as a Vicarage.

Monday, a terrible day, was devoted to washing clothes by hand. By the end of the day, if the Dales housewife had done her work well, her hands would be red and pulpy, her spine on point of shattering and her legs as insensitive as stilts. As she teetered on the verge of prostration, she had the happy knowledge that he had done her work well.

In a big farmhouse like Coat Faw, in Dentdale, soft water was used to prolong the active life of a bar of soap. This water had fallen on the roof of the building as good clean rain, to be collected by guttering and deposited in a cistern made of blue flags, the big pieces being in the tight grip of wrought-iron brackets made by the local blacksmith. Red or white lead sealed the cistern. Naturally, the water was not used for human consumption.

The water was poured into a set-pot, which was a deep metal container for up to 12 gallons, set in a stone structure, with space beneath for a coal or peat fire to be made. Sometimes, it was in an outhouse. Filling the boiler was the very first task on a Monday morning; and lighting a fire beneath it the first of the Monday tasks. The housewife slipped some soap into the water to discourage her husband from using the water, as it warmed, to mix food for the calves.

Dalesfolk once made their own soap. Then they had recourse to a 2lb tin of soft soap from a local shop. Some of the soap was placed in the boiler and the rest in the washer, a tub with a lid and a handle that was worked backwards and forwards to agitate the clothes in warm soapy water. The boiler stood on four legs.

After the wash came the energy-sapping round of ironing and "mending," undertaken in poor light, especially in winter. It went on until the eyes of the women prickled with fatigue.

Horse Power

A N ENTIRE [uncastrated stallion] went on tour to be mated with local mares, but most fell farmers bought in their horses rather than rearing their own. Anthony Bradley remembers his father having a horse called Fanny; she was about 22 years old. The next horse was bought from a grocer at Settle who used to tipple [take groceries round the town] with a horse and cart. The horse he parted with stood about 16 hands and was neither Clydesdale nor Shire. There was no great demand for Shires, which were thought to have too much "feather" and greasy legs.

Jonty Wilson, of Kirkby Lonsdale, liked to shoe horses outside, where any wind blew the smoke away from them. When a horse was being shod for the first time, it was naturally perturbed to suddenly find itself standing in a cloud of acrid fumes as a hot shoe was placed on its foot. Jonty shod horses for sixty years and often remarked that shoeing some animals was "blood for money." If a farmer could get a halter on a young horse that had never been handled; and if he and a couple of friends could pull it to the smithy, by the time Jonty had shod it the animal was half broken in.

He liked the winter afternoons, between four o'clock and knocking off time, then he and the others made a dozen pairs of new shoes ready for future demands. There was no other light in the forge except a bit of gas. It was only a little fish-tail jet. A hunter shoe was completely different from the shoe worn by a horse working on the road. And a timber-hauling horse wore shoes that were different from those used for a farm horse. When Jonty made a shoe he had to combat faults in gait, injuries or diseases of the foot – diseases such as laminitis, side-bone and splits.

James Pratt, auctioneer and cattle dealer in Upper Wensleydale, frequently travelled to Scotland for livestock. His daughter, Annie, drove him to Garsdale by horse and trap so that he might catch the Scotch express at 6 a.m. The horse knew the route even better than the driver. Old Grandfather Pratt was fond of saying: "There'll be men and horses when thee and me's gone."

Annie Mason, of Hawes, remembered some fine horses, including Tim Wiffler, secured from the Middleham trainer, Dobson Peacock, with whom her father was on cordial terms. As a girl, she could not resist riding horses, and she was often sent off to bed for galloping a horse until it was "lathered."

When she rode from Ingleton, over Newby Head, on a foggy day, a phenomenon known as "willie wi' t'wisp" appeared. The horse's mane appeared to shine.

She joined the annual drive of sheep from Wether Fell to wintering quarters at Brimham Rocks, above Nidderdale. "I rode a mare out, then tied the bridle up so that it would not drag, turned the horse round, slapped her on her buttocks, and she returned home of her own accord."

A loveable grey mare had a foal; they were taken to Middleham Moor to be sold and, not being disposed of on the first day, were left there until the second day. That night, Annie cried. She was sure that she would not see them again. "During the night I heard our grey mare come up the paddock at the back of the house. I jumped out of bed and put the window down and shouted out: 'Our old gal's come back'."

She remembers the morning trips to Hawes station with milk floats. The horses knew the routine so well they scarcely needed to be driven. When she and her husband farmed at Gayle, he took the milk float to the station, removed the laden churns and loaded the empties. He turned to talk to a friend. The horse, when it sensed that the empties were in place, set off at a brisk trot, travelling through Hawes, taking the left turn beyond the school for Gayle and drawing up in the yard of the farm. The farmer had to walk home.

The Pratts had the first mowing machine in the area. An old man, seeing the two horses being prepared to draw it across a field, observed:

"Ay, I don't know. Grass'll nivver grow when there's bin a machine on it." Fanny, an old mare, was clever at drawing a mowing machine. If the companion horse was too spirited, Fanny held back. If the other horse did not seem to like work, she kept a good pace going.

The Home Fires

AUTUMN was a busy time at Tan Hill Colliery. It was then that farmers stocked up for the winter. Early in the century, a load of coal, some 8cwt., cost 3s.6d. The visiting farmer paid the "banker" who was on duty at the chute. No one seemed to worry about having a precise quantity. In course of time, no one wanted the coal, for cheaper stuff was available from the deep mines of Durham.

Matthew Cherry was my companion when I visited the remains of one of the best-known of the Tan Hill mines, evident beside the road from West Stonesdale to Tan Hill. It had yielded shiny coal, full of gas that hissed and spluttered in the grate. Combined with peat, it gave an almost savage heat to many a farm and cottage. Matthew had visited the mine often but had never gone underground – at least, on Tan Hill. Bill Alderson, a Swaledale farmer, once joined the miners far from daylight. It was an eerie experience, "as black as t'auld Lad issell. My candle went out an' I lost me cap."

With the native vegetation gone, the wind, rain and frost were making the landscape creep. Hardly any of the entrance to this little mine remained in sight. All we saw were perhaps a dozen stones, forming part of an arch. The bed of the stream had been stained by iron, though water emerging from the mine was clear enough.

We probed the depths under the visible section of arch and did not touch the bottom. Over five feet of water lay in the mouth of the level. It would likely as not be dammed right away up into the sidings as well. When we later chatted with Bill Alderson, he listened intently to our report of this famous old coal mine and said: "There'll be some watter in yonder. If it were let off now, it'd wesh all Swardle away."

This mine was always wet. When Matthew Cherry was last here, after heavy rain, he had stood at the entrance, waiting for the water level to subside. Meanwhile, pieces of rotten timber drifted out. In the old days, a watcher would hear a rumbling sound and see a lile grey pony appear. It was drawing a string of tubs laden with coal. Wet conditions hindered mining. Some farmers left their carts on Tan Hill "aw neet." They rode their horses home and were back next morning, hoping that normal mining had been resumed.

A farmer at the head of Kingsdale bought one cart load of coal in the twenty years he lived in this remote little valley. When he retired to Bentham, he left a bit o' coal in the shed. Most of the time, it was peat that kept the home fires burning. The top peat was mossy. The farther down a man dug, and the harder and darker it became. Bottom peat was nearly as black and hard as coal.

Peat was a cheap fuel that was generally used. The main cost was in effort, not money. "Peat pots" were re-opened in late May or June, after t'cows had been turned out. Old workings were drained so the men were dry when working at a face. If a peat pot was five or six feet deep, digging the stuff was akin to quarrying.

Turves cut by special blades were moved to liggen grund [firm ground] and set up to dry in the sunshine and breezes. When two turves were placed side by side, tilted so they joined at the top, with another peat on top, it was known in Swaledale as a foot and the process was called *pearking*. Peats were later formed into a pike [small stack] for further drying. A Nidderdale farmer reckoned on having 22 peats to a barrow, rather more than 20 barrows to the load and between 50 and 60 loads for the average household. This meant they could burn a load a week – and have one load for luck!

The kindling was often ling sticks, tugged from stretches of moorland that had been fired in spring. Many a load of ling sticks were brought down to the farm by horse and sled. A peat fire left a fine dust on the furniture. The residue from a peat fire fell through a grate into an asshole [ash hole] that was cleaned out as required. At one farm, a muck shovel and two cow buckets were used.

A Dales Haytime

IN JULY, the Dales farmers tapped their barometers with the gusto of a woodpecker at a nesting tree. When one showed "fair" but the weather was extremely bad, he took the barometer into the farmyard, held up the fickle instrument and shouted: "Sitha."

From the rank vegetation came the rasping voice of the corncrake. In those distant days, every field seemed to have a pair of corncrakes. The disyllabic calls of lovelorn cock birds were incessant. If anyone awoke during the night, they had the birds calling by moonlight. It was not easy to get back to sleep as the calls continued.

Haytime was, to quote a Swaledale farmer, blood, sweat and tears. In those pre-Great War days, grass was mown by horse-drawn machine; then the work was done by hand-rake, strawed out, then turned, turned again and "cocked up," being made in such a way the tops would deflect the rain. Then came a week o' wet weather and it had all got to be done again.

Before the mowing machine made its appearance, a common sight was that of a team of men mowing the meadows using huge, long-handled scythes. This was before the Yankee scythe with its curved shaft came into vogue. A man took a new scythe to the blacksmith to have it laid-in [adjusted to his height and style]. Henceforth, no one but the owner must touch the scythe.

An essential part of every straight-shafted scythe was a piece of wood called a strickle, which was pitted with holes, smeared with bacon fat then dusted with a fine, hard sand collected by an upland tarn. This created an abrasive surface and was used to sharpen the blade. A scythesman carried his own grease and sand. Later, the strickle came in a larger size. Its four sides were coated with Emery paper.

A Dales farmer relied on the womenfolk, even some of the children, to do the many tedious haytime jobs like strawing [scattering the mown grass] by hand. "It had to be well spread out. You couldn't get away with chucking it in lumps and leaving bare patches." The workers developed a method of throwing it over their shoulders.

The hay was moved to the barn by horse-drawn sled or a small, two-wheeled cart with shilving [a light wooden frame to extend the cart's capacity]. His father told a young lad with a voracious appetite: "If tha goes on like this, we'll hev to put shilvings on thee plate." At the barn, the forkfuls of hay were removed in reverse order and tossed through the forking-hole. "If the load had been badly put together, there'd be some unParliamentary language."

In 1917, it snowed every day in April and the summer was so cold that men worked in their jackets. If they got to a wallside and had to wait for others to catch up, they were flapping their arms to keep warm. At about that time, a farmer employed two extra men for haytime. One worked for eight weeks and the other for nine weeks. When they left, there was still some hay to be gathered. Only 27 acres of indifferent hay had been put under cover.

Annie Mason told me that when she was a girl on a farm belonging to the Pratt family at Burtersett, she rode a horse that drew a hay-sled to the nearest barn. Grandfather – "a big tall men, with white hair and a white beard" – well knew that work must not take place on Sunday. When darkness fell on a summer Saturday, and there was still hay to be won, he decreed they would work on and get a 'straight edge'. Work went on until midnight and, sure enough, on Sunday afternoon it rained."

If a Dales farmer was not a chapel-man, and therefore teetotal, a barrel of beer would be got in for haytime. There was nothing like a plentiful supply of free ale for attracting workers. Some housewives made herb beer, buying the ingredients and mixing them up at home. It was kept in bottles. If a haytime man asked a young lad to fetch him a bottle, the lad could not resist shaking it to see the cork shoot out. With it went a goodly quantity of ale. The rest went flat. So did the spirits of the man who had asked for it.

Clara Sedgwick, of Dent, told me her father went off to mow with a single-horse mowning machine at 3 a.m., when it was just breaking day. She got up to follow the machine. Mother had made a jug of tea the night before. It was an enamelled jug that now could be heated up. Tea and a bit o' sad cake and 'appen a ginger biscuit or two, was the first of several hayfield snacks. "Our breakfast was coming in a bit – all into t'field. It was a bowl o'porridge, with butter and sugar, and also bacon and egg, if you wanted it. I just had bacon. I was not that fond of eggs. We drank some nice warm tea."

Drinkings [the mid-morning meal] consisted of haverbread and butter, with some home-made cheese and coffee. "We always went home for dinner. It was a right good dinner – a big potato pie and, after that, a pudding of some kind. Or pasties in deep dishes wi' apples. And sometimes roly-poly pudding. We also had a drink o' tea. At tea-time we had jam and bread. If some on 'em wanted cheese, they got cheese and also one of those big plate-pastries and some kind of cake and biscuits.

"After that, we'd have another snack – sandwiches with fried bread and coffee. If t'weather was fine and we were leading [taking hay to the barn], it would appen be half past eleven before we went in at night. For supper, we had some sort o' meat. We'd plenty o' meat. We used to kill our own – lambs or pigs."

At a big farm in upper Wensleydale, two 36-gallon barrels of beer and a bottle of All-Round [a non-alcoholic drink] were purchased. At some farms, the beer was of indifferent quality. As a lad said: "If it was any worse, we couldn't have drunk it, and if it was any better we wouldn't have got it!" At the big farm, only the best was good enough. "We put one barrel of beer into a little square float and had an old mare pulling it. Grandfather passed it round the men at the start of the day."

The farmer's wife and her helpers had to cook for up to 25 men, including workers who were drafted from the quarry into the meadows. Apart from buying in ale, two sheep were slaughtered and some beef was bought from the butcher. She also cooked half a ham. The farmer, who on cattle-dealing travels had stayed at good hotels, would never sit down without a change of plate.

He required a good meal served in the hayfield. "So we used a horse-drawn float to carry a clothes basket with meat, potatoes, gravy in a can, peas and carrots put together; always a pudding, with milk in gill-size bottles and enough crockery to give a change of plate. When the day's work was done, the helpers sat down to a good meal featuring Welsh Rarebit or something like that. The quarrymen liked this. They got better meals than they could afford to make at home." Evidence of the former haytime feasting might be found in drystone walls around the meadows, for any broken crockery was stuffed into cracks and crannies.

A Dales outbarn, which much of the hay was stored, was wonderfully adapted to local conditions – to a fellside culture. Each little barn had a shippon, with tying-up for half a dozen beasts. Hay was stored in the moo [mow] and hay that "worn't fit to go into t'moo" was laid on baulks, above the shippon, where it "nivver got dense enuff to fire."

If the hay in a barn was going to fire, through spontaneous combustion, it did so in about six weeks. A farmer who got his neighbour to keep an eye on the hay while he went on holiday was not amused when that neighbour sniffed the "moo," pronounced the hay of poor quality and said: "A muck-midden nivver fires."

Mutton on the Hoof

THE SHEEP kept in grand-dad's day smelled of tar, which was used for marking them. They were always scratching, which was a consequence of sheep lice. Other sheep, which were maggoted, skulked under cover until they were roused by a dog, to be driven downbank for clipping. This was a job for supermen, who must catch, tug and clip animals that did not want to conform.

A Dales sheep is not ill for long. Either it recovers quickly. Or it dies. The old farmers nivver 'eeard tell of anyone dosing a sheep. Some ailments were wrongly diagnosed. A lamb that was said to have "wool in t'stomach" was suffering from pulpy kidney. "It thrived that fast, its kidneys couldn't cope. Long sin, you lost big lambs – as much as you could carry – and you'd say: 'Oh, well, it's died o' wool in t'stomach'."

Lambs suffering from "drying" had a copper deficiency, though farmers did not know about it then. The lambs went blind and died. From about 1920 the complaint was being cured when a farmer was able to buy an ounce of copper sulphate for a penny; he dissolved it in five pints of water and dosed his sheep – the whole lot, for a penny!

A sheep infested with maggots was treated with paraffin, applied to the affected parts, but it was not satisfactory. A better remedy was Arkle's Magic Maggot Mixture, applied to a sheep with a bit o' cotton. The maggots just dropped off. Maggots thrived in humid conditions. A farmer would say: "It's a right wicking time." They looked for a sheep that was skulking and especially if it had a "dirty behind."

When a sheep got "tremblings," one drastic form of treatment was to get a bicycle pump and blow air into its bag through the teats. An "unthrifty" lamb might have an extra layer of skull, which you tapped and broke with a smooth pebble or the rounded end of a pocket knife; it was known as "skawpin."

Another well-known complaint, sturdy, was caused by a parasite, part of the life-cycle of the tapeworm, that dwelt in a small cyst lodging within the skull. The complaint was said to be caused by the fouling of land by dogs. The affected sheep, disorientated, tended to walk in circles. In the Ingleborough area, sturdy was known as "turn-it-eeard." Mark Kendal, of Newby, was known to be good at the delicate task of "taking a sturdy out." He made a small hole in the skill, then sucked  the little bag out with a goose quill. "You'd see the bag stuck on the quill."

In June, about a fortnight before the sheep were to be clipped, the local beck was dammed, (perhaps with an old door, the sides lagged with sods. The washing places were traditional. Here were handy places where the beck formed a "dub." A sheep that was washed made "rather more" money than the unwashed variety, though as it was a mere thruppence a pound the advantages of washing were slight. In any case, washing wool reduced its weight.

Washing sheep rid the fleece of grease and dirt picked up from the peat hags. As the number of sheep washed in a day might be 3,000, from several farms, not much attention could be paid to an individual sheep. You would be forgiven for thinking that the man was in the dub simply to make sure the sheep didn't get out too soon.

In Swaledale, two men stood up to their chests in water and "weshed" the sheep as someone threw them in on the bank. A man would "riffle" the wool up and turned t'sheep ower to wesh in between the legs and across its belly. If there was an especially mucky sheep – one that was clarted up at its rump – a chap would shout, as he chucked it into t'watter: "Gie it a good do – it's a mucky 'un." The sheep was released and thankfully staggered on to dry land.

Washing day was jolly for the men, except the luckless ones who had to spend an hour or so up to their chests in cold water. It was not jolly for the sheep. A meal was brought up from the handiest farm. There'd be boiled ham, hard-boiled eggs and haverbread. Home-brewed beer – strong stuff – was popular. At some spots, there'd be sports for the kids.

Grease went into t'beck. Fish came up, gasping for air. Some of the lads would pick up fish but, tainted with tar and grease, they no longer tasted of fish.

Clipping day was a grand day. Ivverybody had a good laugh. Owd-fashioned jokes were flying around. Women made sandwiches. The farmer's wife made a big tatie pie. Tea was served in big cans. In Dentdale, the old uns remembered the "boon" days when neighbours assisted each other with the clipping of sheep. Lads were set to work catching sheep. The same lads would put fresh marks on them when the fleeces had been removed. Tar was used for re-marking until the wool-combers complained.

The old way of clipping was to put a sheep on t'stock and tie three feet. Doing this, a man could clip a sheep in t'time some men would spend waiting for it to stop fidgetting. A sheep that was clipped too closely might get "hill-chilled" in bad weather.

In autumn, the sheep were sorved [salved], a fleece being parted in sheds [lines] and a mixture of tar and grease applied to the skin. This custom began to decline after 1905, when a compulsory dipping order was introduced. The salver sat on a creel and got his salve from a small dish which could be fitted to the creel.

All the wool, including tails and toppings, was parted. Attending to "tails and toppings" was usually left to the lads when they got back from school. The "sheds" were about an inch apart and the salve was applied to the skin with a finger. Archangel or Stockholm tar – and sometimes an American tar – were available from a local dealer, such as Matthew Sedgwick of Sedbergh. He could also supply the grease, though some farmers used home-produced butter that had gone rancid. Good butter was available at sixpence a pound.

One type of grease was called Black Jack. In Swaledale, a farmer used a mixture of brown grease, whale oil and tar. The brown grease was "sad, still and stiff" but it was mellowed when it came in contact with the whale oil.

When making salve, you had not to get it too hot or the salve would be too hard to use. The salve was said to protect the wool and kill lice – "them lile flat lice called kades." Put too little tar into t'salve and you'd be terribly bothered with kades. Put too much in, and you would burn the wool. You had to blend it carefully.

Salving was prolonged. Work went on after dark, when lanterns were lit or the candles were stuck on suitable ledges in the outbuildings, for the work was done under cover. It got nice and warm when you were shut up wi' a lot o' sheep. Sometimes, t'smell o' tar and grease made me sick. I'd get up to oppen t'door and let a bit more air in."

1910-1919

The 1914-18 war shattered the social fabric and slaughtered many fine young dalesmen. At Kettlewell, stained glass windows were designed to commemorate the sons of two local families. Men who served overseas and returned to the Dales found that farmers who "med a bit" during t'war had "summat in t'bank." Newcomers to farming were badly hit by the Slump. After a year's hard work, one couple lost £2,000. A farmer's son who swallowed a silver coin was taken to the local parson, who was reputed to be able to "get brass out of anybody."

In Time of War

THE GREAT WAR was a day or two old before the news percolated to the remotest farms and hamlets. It reached the straddling, moorside community of Keasden, near Clapham, as an item of gossip picked up from a tramp. The well-to-do exhorted ordinary folk to greater efforts by knitting mufflers and mittens for t'lads at the Front. At Ingleborough Hall, Clapham, Mrs Farrer mustered her staff and local ladies and was photographed with them; she held a Union Jack.

Dales conscripts were usually bagged by the Duke of Wellington's Regiment, which was widely known as the Havercake Lads after their partiality for oatcake. A Dales milkman, approached by a recruiting sergeant, was asked if he wished to serve the King and said: "Aye – but I can nobbut spare one pint today." Apart from the relief funds set up to provide shirts and socks, eggs were collected for hospitals, who also received heaps of dried sphagnum moss, to be used for dressings.

As the war rumbled on, and young soldiers were dying amid the mud of Flanders, the Settle Board of Guardians discussed whether or not it was possible to tell margarine from butter by tasting. Mr Harger had raised the question of the substitution of margarine for butter at the workhouse. He pointed out that margarine was now extensively used. The people who did use it said they could hardly tell which was which.

Mr Charlesworth said that three or four years ago when butter was 18d a pound – presumably this was a wholesale price, though the difference would be little more than a penny – four butter-dealers were recruited to test it out. They were confident they could recognise good butter but unwittingly gave the first prize to margarine. No one consulted the inmates. Naturally, for the change from butter to margarine would save £200 a year.

To be farming in the Dales in 1917 was only marginally butter – er, better – than Flanders. Or so some of the farmers said during the first eighteen days of April, when it snowed, and for most of a miserable summer, when it was wet and blowy. Those who had to plough up good grassland to grow corn found the crop did not ripen under the lead-grey skies. When cut, the stuff rotted in the sheaves. The smell of rotting corn hung over the lower dale-country. Old folk said the bad weather was caused by all the gunfire in France.

At a Ribblesdale farm, a new strain of sheep evolved during that frightful year. The farmer at a moor-edge holding filled his house and outbuildings with refugee sheep and lambs. When one yow and her offspring remained, in desperation he pushed them into the outside toilet, known as a privvy. Henceforth, this strain was known as "them privvy sheep."

The war drew wearily to an end. An uneasy peace ensued. Old soldiers never died; they regaled their cronies with tales of conflict. Old Mick, the bull-walloper, who had been bayonetted in the throat at the Battle of Mons, claimed to have seen the apparition known as the Angel of Mons.

One dalesman was left with one good leg and one wooden leg. The joint became uncomfortable when the wood swelled with a change of weather. The lad sandpapered his wooden limb from time to time in a policy that could not last forever.

Writing from his "mountain home" at Malham Tarn House, Walter Morrison brought some words of comfort to Mr George Jenkinson, of the Black Horse at Giggleswick, who had lost his son on active service. "You must feel that he could not have given his life for a nobler cause." It was "Morrison money" that defrayed much of the expense of providing a special welcome home to the Servicemen in August, 1919.

From the same source came money for a book in which those who served were listed, many with photographs, thus prolonging the grief.

Butter and Cheese

A T CAW FAW, in upper Dentdale, in the days before margarine became commonplace, the Middletons had a thriving herd of milk cows. Well, about thirteen cows was t'average in summer. It was just as well that Mr Middleton was not superstitious. With two milkings a day, and everything done by hand, the Middletons must have got weary of contemplating the "bag" and tits of bovine stock.

Occasionally, a weary cow enlivened its day by kicking over the bucket of milk or drawing its tail across the face of the milker. Embedded in the hair of the tail were hard bits of dung, known to bleeding farmers as "muck buttons."

Most of the milk was poured into shallow metal containers with sloping sides and left until the cream had separated and was clinging to the sides. Then a plug was withdrawn, the "blue" milk was drawn off, and – using a piece of horn – the cream was scraped off the metal and kept in a crock. Some of it was made into butter and some became the basis of cheese. The "blue" milk was given to the farm men or t'pigs.

On butter-making day, the crock was emptied of soured cream, which was churn until the person turning the handle felt it judder or hear the *slap, slap* of butter hitting the sides. At Caw Faw, mother had poor health. She got her sons to turn the handle, sometimes while singing *Onward Christian Soldiers*, which was just the right speed.

When the young daughter returned from school, where she was taught how to add up, she weighed the butter which, a pound at a time, was "worked" in a wooden bowl to form "round pounds" for sale.

Chunky Parkinson, who had a horse and cart, collected the stuff from Dent. In some weeks, 80 lb of butter left this one farm.

Cheese-making was widespread in the Dales. It must have been made by the Norse folk who had their winter homes in the dales and their summer grazings on the hills, where it would be expedient to lock up the goodness of summer milk as cheese that could be consumed during the winter. When commerce reared its head, the best cheese was sold to townsfolk. Cheese made with "blue" milk, and known as whangby, was given to those with strong jaws. It could be so hard it must be attacked with an axe. Even the mice turned their noses up at it.

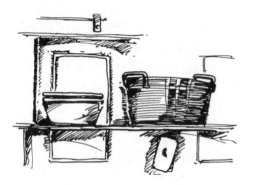

Wensleydale gave its name to the Dales type of cheese. By the time of the Great War, factory production had been operating for half a century but cheese was still being made at farms, using – so it was said – a recipe given to the dalesfolk by the monks of Jervaulx Abbey, who brought the cheese-making skills from France. At least, it made a good story...

At one farm, about three o' clock on a September day, the womenfolk would begin to turn 100 gallons of milk into cheese. The milk had to be kept at blood-heat so the containers were placed on a hessian mat that had been stuffed with straw. After the rennet was added to the milk, the vat was covered with two oak boards and the whole wrapped in a rug to keep it warm.

In an outer kitchen were the big iron cheese presses, each having a suspended stone to exert pressure. The room where the cheeses were stored after pressing was fitted with wooden shelves. The cheeses were turned every day and the shelves washed down once a week. The cheese from this farm was transported to Mr Leyland, a grocer at Bainbridge, in a milk float that had been strewn with straw so that the big cheeses would not be bruised. Three big cheeses lay on end, covered with a woollen rug, and Mr Leyland consigned them to Manchester or Liverpool.

A Nip o' Summat Strong

A DALES farmer, confined to the house by the common cold, let everybody know he was ill. He sat by the fire, head sunk, moaning intermittently. His wife responded by bringing him the universal cure – a nip o' spirits, medicine for man or beast. It was said in non-Methodist families that a generous helping of gin or whiskey would stop a cold. The stuff that came from the doctor did little more than shift t'phlegm and didn't get to t'main spot.

Doctors charged for their services, which is not surprising. They were at everybody's beck and call at all times. The summons to the loneliest farms was usually just after milking time at night

In the wild old days, when liquor was cheap, a shepherd went out and about at lambing time with a flask of spirits. It saved at least one chap's life. In a sudden blizzard, he and his dogs had gathered sheep on the fell and brought them into one of the home pastures. He was "all in" but remembered his lile bottle of whisky. Crouching behind a wall, fighting for his breath, he forced his chilled fingers to undo the top buttons on his coat and then quested for the bottle.

He could not manage to uncork it, so he smashed the neck of the bottle against the wall and poured the hot liquid down his throat. The sensation was like someone ramming a hot poker down his throat but it stimulated him enough to enable him to cover the last short distance to the farmhouse.

A Keasden haytime was made notable by the discovery, among the Irish labourers, of a champion distiller of spirits. He was told to concentrate on that. The others would do the hay-making. A shopping list prepared by the Irishman was soon dealt with. The home-made still was kept in a loft in the barn for many years.

Folk 'at's tired gits childish
An' starts t'owd world disorders –
There'd be less quarrels if they grew
Wallflowers i' their borders.

Dorothy Una Ratcliffe.

1920-29

A Craven farmer bought his first car for £3. It had a "dicky seat" at the back. He got a joiner to replace it with a box and toured the local villages, selling meat. Dick Guy started a bus service in Swaledale in 1920, using an old Seabrook lorry, a flat-bottomed vehicle on which rows of seats were fitted. In the late 1920s, Young Farmers' Clubs were breaking down the native shyness and reserve of dalesfolk. It was known for a lad from one dale to court a lass from the next, which had nivver been 'eard of in olden time. Women's Institutes had become a vibrant force in rural affairs.

On Four Wheels

THE STORY of how the first Model T Ford reached Cam Houses, at the headwaters of the Wharfe, was told to me by Kit Calvert. It seems that a member of the Lambert family, known as Bob o' Cams, was fond of ale. It was he who visited Hawes for the shopping and when there was any livestock trading. Drinking something stronger than lemonade was part of the attraction.

When the Model T Ford appeared in Wensleydale, Bob met an agent in Hawes. Bob being short o' brass, he reasoned that if he showed some interest in the Tin Lizzie, the agent my treat him to a drink. The agent paid for a pint and Bob said he would take delivery of the car and pay for it when it was delivered to the door of his home at Cam Houses.

The agent did his best. He drove through Gayle and up the drag to Fleet Moss, the highest stretch of motor road in Yorkshire. The car jibbed somewhere along the three and a-half miles of rough track, a cul de sac, and stopped, axle deep in mud a mile above the remote settlement. The agent admitted defeated and sorrowfully drove the car slowly back to Hawes.

The country garage had become established in the 1920s, the garageman taking over many of the tasks that had previously been carried out by the blacksmith. Fred Ellis, a pioneer garageman at Settle, had a notable customer – the local millionaire, Walter Morrison of Malham Tarn House. It was difficult to persuade him to exchange his horse and carriage for a Fiat car and the day when this occurred was traumatic for his 75-year-old coachman.

In the morning he had reins in his hand as he drove the outfit down to Settle. Here the short-tempered Billy Slinger, kicked the coachman's foot off the clutch to get the car started and gave him a quick course on how to drive a car. It was left to the coachman to drive up the steep brow to Malham Moor. Only once did the erstwhile coachman forget himself – and that was as he approached the gate to the stable yard. He shouted: *whooooa*. The car did not stop when commanded; it was slightly damaged as it grazed some masonry.

Private motoring was slow to develop. If a Dales farmer speculated on a car, it was usually second-hand. Some men taught themselves how to drive using a Land Car, usually an old Austin, that was being adapted for use in the hayfield. One Land Car was provided with a ledge at the front for a kit of water that was to be used to top-up the radiator.

Rufus Carr, of Rimington, specialised in making Land Cars. He would strip down an old Austin and attach to it an ordinary farm mowing machine, the sort drawn by horses, but now minus the shaft. The machine was henceforth to be chain-driven from the back axle of the car. There was scepticism among local farmers, who – on the day it was to be tested out – reckoned they were not interested but skulked behind a hedge to watch the proceedings. They were soon ordering Land Cars of their own.

The Austin 12 was a favourite, being heavy, with a four cylinder petrol engine. Rufus bought a car from a scrapyard for as little as 17s.6d and the modification was carried out with the help of a lad. Rufus's sister-in-law tested out each vehicle before delivery. A Land Car made in the 1920s and sold for £17 was still in use throughout the 1939-45 war.

Rufus produced the equivalent of a small-farm tractor when he put two gear-boxes on an old Austin car. The efficiency was increased when two tyres were used on each of the back wheels. The normal tyre had another fitted over it, the wire rim of the additional tyre having been removed and slots made to provide extra "grip."

In the late 1920s, the departure of the first orange-painted Pennine bus from Skipton to Ingleton was timed to be convenient for a Gargrave lady who taught at Coniston Cold school. The rest of the timetable was arranged around this appointment. No official bus stops existed. When it was market day at Settle, farmers' wives clambered aboard with butter baskets. It was known to a farmer, en route for Skipton auction mart, to board the bus with a newly-born calf swaddled in sacking.

The driver collected prescriptions at Dr Lovegrove's surgery at Settle, then went on to Shepherd and Walker, the chemists, to have them made up. Fish and chips were ordered by villagers who met the 9 p.m. bus out of Skipton. The driver would collect the delicacies from John Andrews's shop in the Shambles at Settle for distribution on the return journey.

High quality cars, including Bentleys and Bugati's, raced in competition up the Banks from Pateley Bridge to Greenhow Hill. When a man was knocked down, a driver picked him up, dusted him down, and asked what he might do as compensation. The bemused pedestrian, facing a new situation, simply replied: "How much do you normally pay?"

Unwillingly to School

A TYPICAL Dales village school, a hangover from Victorian times, had two rooms. Light was admitted by tall lancet windows, infilled with obscured glass. While at their lessons, the children must have no distractions from the outer world. The smaller classroom was for "infants" and the later accommodated the other children, right up to the age of eleven.

No nonsense was tolerated and the cane was in general use. Major J E E Yorke, of Halton West, chatted with a man who, after telling of the teacher at his school, in days long ago, remarked: "She put us through t'small sieve." A new boy was excused when he was seen to be crying. The teacher asked his best friend what was the matter. He said: "He's dug a hole and he wants to take it into school."

A Dentdale lad was the envy of his friends when he had only two days' schooling. His family were "takkin' t'fell in" and he had to sheep-watch. As he put it, "I mun keep t'yows in t'reight place."

The other children went to school from five till 14. At the edge of human memory were days punctuated by the squeak of pencils against slates.

A self-confessed dunce said, after he had spent years "doing sums an' writin', wi a bit o' drawin' and a bit o' paintin' and sich like," that he could not read. "They could nivver bray owt into my 'eeard, tha knaws." As a truant, he was sought by the attendance officer, who was known locally as t'whipper in.

Farm children had long walks to school, their clogs ringing on the roads. They carried a few sandwiches and a lile bit o' sad cake for their mid-day meal. "It was nowt special. When I'd eaten up, I washed it down wi' cowd water from t'tap in t'schoolyard."

Children mustered in neat lines in the playground and marched into school. Three R's – Reading, Riting and Rithmatic (four, if you added Religion) – were the backbone of the syllabus. There was a little bit of science when a teacher produced two little baking tins, one empty and one holding water. She the produced a sponge. A farmer's lad, suspecting what was going to happen, picked up the sponge, put it in the water and squeezed the water into the other tin. The teacher was vexed for he had spoilt her lesson.

At Bainbridge, the children had an hour's Scripture, for a start. It was like being in church. Hardraw had teachers who really cared and offered a variety of lessons, including singing and sewing, crocheting and knitting on four needles. They would not tolerate ill manners and if a boy swore he would be taken into the porch so his mouth could be washed out, using carbolic soap.

One of the "fancy" subjects was art. A lile lad from a dalehead farm was having difficulty with the sky on a picture entitled "My Home." The helpful schoolmistress showed him how to paint a sky and did so with lots of blue and with big, fluffy clouds. He looked disdainfully at it and remarked: "Nay, miss – where I come from, t'sky's allus mucky."

When a teacher drew the letter S on the blackboard and asked a boy what it was, he surprised her by saying: "A door sneck."

Farmer's Boy

THE aforementioned Major Yorke, whose Ribblesdale estate extended along the west bank of the river at Halton West, recalled that when the early post-war boom had gone and conditions were bad, he took on a farm man, who had a wife and two children. They had previously been paid 28s, plus the tenancy of a house. An old Dales shepherd had told him of the days when his father and mother brought up five children in such poverty "we were hungered."

It was a hard time for farm men. They had no set number of hours. There were no days off: it was a seven-days-a-week job. On hiring day, in the market town, a knot of men gathered at a central point and were approached by farmers who wanted men. In a good many cases, labourers were taken on privately.

Every man desired a farm where the housewife was a good cook. Farmhouse food has been romanticised in rural books. All too often, farm fare was dire. And frugal. Jonty Wilson, helping out as a lad on a farm in Chapel-le-Dale, soon discovered that meal-times were indicated by the ringing of a bell. On the first day, when the rush to the kitchen began, a man tripped up. Jonty helped him to his feet. Valuable time had been lost. The man thanked him and said: "There's not much point in going for dinner now. There'll be nowt left."

A Ribblesdale farmer hired a man who had served in the 1914-18 war, paying him £60 for the half year, with his keep. It was an enormous wage by the standards of the time. Not long afterwards, as the slump came, wages dropped back. Ten shillings a week was a common wage in the 1920s and the only time off for a holiday was Whitsuntide and Martinmas. A farmer who offered a man 15s a week told him to keep the sum to himself. The other men were getting 14s.

A lad hired at a Dentdale farm worked 26 weeks and was paid £20. "I hadn't wanted farm work. It was hard work. But there was nothing else. Dad said: 'Well, you'll have to start doing summat. I can't keep you here.' He went across the dale to a farmer friend. When he came back, he handed me a shilling. I was hired. Mother gave me my stuff in a tin box. I had some fustian breeches, clogs, an old shirt or two. It was work. I pretended I was enjoying myself. I hated it."

The farm man, "a second pair of hands," was considered by some farmers to be "fit for nowt but wark – strong in t'back an' weak in t'heeard." Most of them were regarded as one of the family, ate at the same time and sat up to the fire with them in the evening.

An exception was the farmer near Horton-in-Ribblesdale who paid a man £14 a year "with all found" and imposed a strict regime. None of his men was to enter the farmhouse, whatever the weather, apart from meal-times and shortly before it was time to go to bed. In winter, the hired man warmed his hands by placing them on the backs of cows. At another farm in the upper valley, the hired chap rose at 5 a.m. in summer and at 6 a.m. in winter. Before breakfast, he was called upon to milk and fodder the beasts. In winter he must not carry a candle or a paraffin lamp. The farmer said that such items were uneconomical.

Wages were negotiable. There was no prescribed time for ending work. A farm man's best course of action was to marry the farmer's daughter. One lad from poor parents was in effect being kept for learning about farming. Usually, a man worked for six or seven years – then found a small farm to rent and went on till he had a farm of his own.

Run, Rabbit, Run

RABBITS kept many a Dales family alive in hard times. In the 1920s, when a rabbit skin was worth a shilling, rabbits might also pay the rent. M'duke Miller of Littondale recalled when rabbit-catchers on the larger Dales farms were bagging anything from 3,000 to 5,000 rabbits in a season. He had been talking to a catcher who said he made £400 for rabbits in one season. A rabbit warren in Kingsdale, near Ingleton, lay on a bracken-covered hillside and was isolated by a wire fence. Rabbits were flushed out with the use of ferrets.

Rabbits competed with the cattle and sheep on the grazings. When the Hodgson family arrived at Tennant Gill, on Malham Moor, the first problem was to dispose of hungry bunnies. At first, only 16 cattle could be kept. When war was waged on the rabbits, there was eatage for 80 cattle.

The men who diligently put out snares and made regular rounds of them might catch 500 rabbits a week. By the late 1930s, rabbit catching was not profitable. Phyllis Kelway, the naturalist-writer, spent some days watching rabbits at close quarters in Appletreewick. She marked down some suitable burrows for photography. "Unfortunately, the week-end brought armies of hikers to the rabbit field. After their tumult and shouting had died, I returned to the quiet field to watch again my favourite burrows. No rabbits appeared."

She investigated and found that the holes had been stuffed with old saucepans, kettles, two pairs of stockings, an electric bulb bowl and – a suspender belt.

Total Eclipse

IN 1927, Giggleswick was mentioned so often in the press that the magazine *Punch* began to publish amusing notes about the name. It was all to do with the total eclipse of the sun. An estimated 100,000 people crowded into the area in the early hours of June 29. It was the first time for two centuries that the phenomenon would be visible in this country and the Astronomer Royal, Sir Frank Dyson, set up his camera to record the few seconds when day became night.

A man who saw the Giggleswick spectacular recalls: "We were told this would be the sight of a lifetime. There'd be nowt like it in t'country for a hundred years. Now, if I wanted, I could travel down to Cornwall this August and see it again. I'm too old to bother."

Sir Frank and his party were to be found not far from the celebrated domed chapel of Giggleswick School which itself had been taken for an astronomy. Those who stared hard at it hoped to see a telescope sticking from the dome. (Another likened the chapel to a jelly mould!).

Sir Frank, questioned shortly after the eclipse, thought it was perhaps as much as three seconds early. "The corona was bright…Four or five red prominences were distinctly seen…Some observers in our enclosures saw streamers of the corona extending to one and a half diameters of the sun."

My old friend Stan Potts recalled seeing the eclipse from the hill immediately behind the railway station at Horton-in-Ribblesdale, where many of those who arrived by special train assembled. Others stood on Moughton Fell, but those climbing Penyghent lost themselves in cloud and saw – nowt! Back at Horton, Billy Bentham, who farmed Rowe End, heated up water in a set-boiler, then transferred it to a back-can along with a quarter of a pound of tea. Wearing the back-can and

holding a basket full of cups and mugs, he dispensed tea to the sun-gaz-
ers. The demand for "summat hot" greatly exceeded the supply. At
Hellifield, to the south, the sky was clear and the experience of totality,
when no birds sang and no one spoke, was distinctly eerie.

The couple who farmed Colt Park, at the top of Ribblesdale, climbed
Park Fell, part of the Ingleborough group and were cloudbound. They
returned sorrowfully to the farmyard, only to see the eclipse clearly
from their back door. For a man who joined a throng on a steep hillside
above the Settle-Langcliffe high road, the quietness of an enormous
crowd was impressive.

The Foggitt family of Thirsk got no nearer than Leyburn, in
Wensleydale, because of the press of vehicles. Seeing the eclipse
prompted Bill Foggitt to study the weather. He became a well-known
amateur forecaster.

Onyx Ralph, out and about with a party from Settle Girls' High
School, had a good view of the eclipse. In the school log it was recorded: "Seventy-eight children from Standards IV to VIII met at school at
4.20 a.m. today and were taken by the full staff to Spen Pasture, an
observation field behind Giggleswick Chapel, to witness a total eclipse
of the sun at 6.23 a.m. and of 23 seconds duration. After a cloudy
beginning, an excellent view was obtained of the total eclipse, the corona and the huge flames. The last vestige of eclipse vanished at 7.23 a.m.,
when the children were sent home until the opening of school at 9 a.m."

Boys and teachers from Central High School left Leeds station in a
special train at 1 a.m. and after a slow journey the train drew into the
platform at Clapham station about daybreak. The eclipse was observed
from a large field to the south of the village. The party then climbed
Ingleborough.

At 4 a.m., dense crowds packed the town of Settle. An observer who
saw special trains arriving said: "It was like watching a mass migra-
tion." It had been hoped that the Prince of Wales, who was staying
overnight at Witherslack Hall, near Morecambe Bay, would visit
Giggleswick to view the eclipse but, being told that the weather was
bad, he stayed in bed.

Ah see, Spring's getten here yance mair,
An' winter's owered, Ah declare …
Neea peece for neeabody, Ah seear!
For t'wimmin's getten t'cleanin' fit,
You canna find a spot to sit.

Elsie A Grassby.

1930-1939

In 1931, top lambs made about £2 each. A year later they were down to 30s and in 1933, the price was 17s.3d. Motor-bikes were more common than cars and many a farmer had nothing more elaborate than a push-bike. The Milk Marketing Board came into being in 1933 and gave the farmer the benefit of regular collections and a monthly cheque. Previously, many milk producers had consigned their milk by train to a city like Bradford or Leeds. Payment was irregular if at all. The coming of the Youth Hostels' Association in 1930 provided ordinary folk with good but cheap accommodation in straitened times.

The Lean Years...

RENT DAYS were a torment to landlord and tenant alike. Benny Taylor, agent for the Ings Estate, which owned some of the best land round Hawes, organised his rent day at the Crown Hotel. Jack Chapman told him: "I 'ev nowt. You 'ev nowt. So there's nowt for noan on us. I'll do thee some walling to cover t'rent." The offer was accepted. When Old Tommy and Jenny Taylor, of Hawes, received their first 7s.6d under a national pension scheme, they thought that Heaven had opened. They had a regular income – for life!

In the 1930s, a sheep was not ill for long. "It awther got better – or it deed." Medicine came out of a bottle. If the farmer was feeling under the weather, he might surreptitiously have a swig.

A Dales family did not think of sending for a doctor unless his presence was vital. He charged for his services. In lean times, the doctor's invoice was given priority over other debts that had to be met. A Wensleydale woman who had double-pneumonia when she was four years old dimly recalls that her mother and Aunt Bessie sat up with her.

"My brother had pneumonia each March for three years in succession. Dr Grimes told us that his schooling did not matter; he had to live an open-air farm life, with plenty of good food. We took the window panes from his bedroom. When he was delirious, we had to hold him down. He grew up into a big strong chap."

Infections like scarlet fever were handled at isolation hospitals. There was one at Bainbridge, in Wensleydale. Local people called it the "fever house." They kept away from it. Fresh air was prescribed for whooping cough. In Craven, an ailing child would be taken to the lime kilns and told to inhale fumes off the lime. Billy Chapman, of Wensleydale, had an unusual remedy for whooping cough. He boiled a mouse and gave the juice of it to any suffering child.

Dr Anderton, of Hawes, bled people, cutting into a vein with a knife. Powder from a puff ball was said to seal a wound. Spiders' webs would stop bleeding. In a bid to stay healthy, most people ate the crust off the cheese, complete with any mould that had formed. Poulticing was commonly practised for such ailments as bronchitis. The customary way of making a poultice was to cut an old blanket into oblongs. Boiling water was poured on to linseed meal, a mixture was made and it was "plastered" on the blanket, "like jam on to bread." If the skin of the sufferer was smeared with olive oil before the poultice was applied, the skin would never blister.

The most celebrated Dales doctor was Will Pickles, of Aysgarth, who knew and was known by every person in the dale and served them wondrously for over half a century. He also made a major contribution to our medical knowledge.

He moved from Leeds to Wensleydale at a time when remote farms were visited on horseback and emergency operations performed on kitchen tables by the light of candles and hurricane lamps. A patient heard a doctor's assistant say he'd never seen an anaesthetic given before and remarked, between tears, "Let's not bother wi' chloroform. Get on wi' t'operation and put me out o' this pain."

He was fascinated by the spread of infection, often along the bus route through the dale. He published his findings on what he called (and is still called) "farmer's lung," which resulted from repeated inhalation of dust from mouldy hay. His great friend Fred Lawson, the artist, said of Dr Will: "He stops and chats and gives confidence. That's what a lot of these old people want. You'd be surprised how much medicine ends up down the sink."

Let there be Light!

THE INN on Tan Hill, even in the 1930s, Susan Peacock had to make do with oil lamps. Yet the 1930s saw the introduction of electricity to many Dales villages. Jim Ward bought the waterwheel from the "flagworks" at Helwith Bridge and used it to generate electricity for a few properties in Horton-in-Ribblesdale.

It was in the early 1930s that electricity arrived in Malhamdale. To justify the expense of wiring-up homes at the dalehead, the electricity company specified they would begin the work only if a dozen local people subscribed. It was an effort to find them. Dales caution prevailed. Nearly everyone wanted to wait and benefit from the experiences of those who rushed to have it installed. It was a matter of: "We'll see how them goes on 'at gets it."

Thomas Geldard, one of the first 12 customers, had four electric lights installed downstairs and he and his family still went to bed by candlelight. Mrs Geldard was seen downstairs with a candle. She was frightened to switch on the electricity because of the expense. An electrician called at a cottage where lights were ablaze in the middle of the afternoon. The owner exclaimed: "I like t'electric. Doesn't it last a long time?" Another consumer said: "They've put t'electric in lile glass bottles. I can neither turn it down nor blow it out!"

At Clapham, in 1935, the Settle Electricity Company was supplying power for a penny a unit. The village had a pioneering system of electrical generation. The Farrers, having dammed up Clapdale to create Ingleborough Lake, later used a turbine to generate electricity for selected buildings, including those at the nearby woodyard, and for street lighting. I lodged with the Shaw family at the Woodyard Cottage. An evening ritual was "switching on the street lights." A short time before I had lodged with Hetty Turner at a house which reeked of paraffin, used for lighting, heating and cooking.

Boots, Bikes and Buses

B Y THE mid-1930s, the Dales had been discovered by the working class ramblers and cyclists of the northern towns. Tom Stephenson, champion of ramblers' rights, met two American girls. They told him they had trudged along the 2,000 miles of the Appalachian Trail, in the eastern United States, and inquired from him if something of the sort existed in England. Stephenson suggested they might follow a route along the Pennines and, a journalist, he returned to the subject in an article he wrote for the *Daily Herald* on June 22, 1935.

[It was the germ of the idea that led in 1951 to the designation of the Pennine Way, then the longest continuous footpath in Britain, extending for 250 miles from Edale in Derbyshire to Kirk Yetholm in Scotland. Many are content to walk just one section. The most popular is the 55 miles from Gargrave to the Tan Hill Inn. The Pennine Way was officially opened in 1965].

In 1938, Alfred Wainwright of Blackburn set out on a Long Walk. He wrote about his experiences, tucked the manuscript away, brought it out in recent times, when he had become famous for his hand-written, hand-drawn guides to the Lake District, and it was published in 1986. He climbed Penyghent, exulting mightily; he crossed Foxup Moor, finding "a confusion of sheep-tracks to bewilder the traveller."

CTC – these were the well-known initials of the Cyclists' Touring Club, whose emblem featured silver wings. Donald Lee, of Keighley, was one of those intrepid cyclists who pedalled up t'Dales in an hour or two and called at one of t'CTC places for a pot of tea. It cost fourpence. Weary cyclists returning home might call at the Post Office at Malham, where Mrs Brown made an especially claggy fruit cake. This staved off "hunger knock" and its dreaded successor, "bonk," which reduced a cyclist to prostration.

The *CTC Handbook* was the touring cyclist's bible. In the early 1930s, a cyclist who wanted bed and breakfast was in competition with the driver of an Austin Seven. He belonged to the AA but carried the cyclists' handbook. "If you saw him, you'd beat him to it." From 1930 there were youth hostels available; the basic charge was a shilling a night.

The cyclists of the 1920s had toured on "ten bob a day." Rather more was needed in the 1930s yet cycling was still a relatively cheap way for young people from the milltowns to have a stimulating break from the home routine. A summer run for some began at 6 a.m. from "under the clock" at the old Mechanics' Institute in Keighley. "When the clock struck six, those of us who were there – went! If anyone was late, they'd to catch us up."

The "toughies" swept up the dales and stormed the fells, stopping at cyclist "tea shops" such as Mrs Falshaw's at Buckden or "open house" kept by Sam Stables and his wife at Grassington. "You never let them know you were coming, but they were never caught without food if you popped in." It was known for Mrs Stables to rise from her bed at 5-30 a.m. on a Sunday to make Cornish pasties and cakes.

Buses, which had a greater mobility than the railways, had their golden age in the Dales during the 1930s. The Wensleydale bus had a driver and conductor, pneumatic tyres, two doors – both on the nearside – and a long rope by which the bell was rung. On market days, passengers arrived with poultry hampers, eggs and rabbits. At Howgill Bank, Askrigg, the passengers had to walk and the bus was "chocked" yard by yard, as it roared slowly uphill.

It was on a Pennine bus, from Clapham to Skipton, that I studied the conversation between two farmers sitting on the next seat. One man was quite a chatterbox. The other said little beyond "aye," which he uttered with variations of speed, pitch and inflection. By the time the bus reached Skipton, he had said "aye" ninety-nine times and, from the manner of his friend, he had made an intelligent contribution to the discussion.

Rich winter smells of loam and muddy lanes,
Of heath and snow and frost and ponderous rains.
Breathe deep, breathe deep.

Amy Jackson.

1940-1949

A good lambing-time paid the farm rent for three years. In a bad lambing-time, the Dales farmer tightened his belt in anticipation of hard times. Cold and wet meant that lambs were chilled. One way of reviving a "starved" lamb was to administer a drop of spirit from a whisky flask. The same treatment was prescribed for a chilled farmer. With the nation at war, machines invaded the landscape. When the war ended, they proved to be easier and far more interesting to employers than the old, toilsome ways. Italian and German prisoners-of-war who helped on the farms had the opportunity to be repatriated. Some Germans married Dales lasses.

Tractors and Land Girls

YOUNG LADIES of the Women's Land Army – the so-called Land Girls – moved into a Dales landscape and helped to turn it "brown side up." Farmers grunted and growled. T'land wasn't suited to growing oats and fancy root crops like Red King taties and swedes.

Come to think of it – t'land wasn't quite ready for lasses in pants. Or so it was thought till one or two of those lasses married into farming and changed their minds. Initially, these lasses from t'towns had a lot to learn. One of them, having driven a tractor to a garage, explained what had gone wrong and added: "When whatever-it-was went, it was just like a shoulder-strap snapping."

That Land Girl was in her working togs – bib and brace dungarees, black boots or gunboots. You'd have scarcely recognised her if you'd seen her at some social event, for then she would be resplendent in a green pullover, corduroy knee-breeches, fawn knee-length stockings and brown leather shoes. This eye-turning outfit was completed by a three-quarter length brown overcoat.

Some Land Girls mastered the skills of working with horses but mainly it was tractors that drew the ploughs that shredded the old grasslands of the Dales. As mentioned, Dales farmers didn't care for ploughs. They considered it would have been better for t'war effort if t'fields had been left sprouting grass. Their pleas went unheeded.

The War-Ag [War Agricultural Committee] arranged a rota of ploughing on every farm. The Ministry man shuffled some forms. The tractors and ploughs moved in and tore up the landscape. Workers were always pushed for time, 'cept when there was a cup of tea in the offing. Or perhaps a ham sandwich from a home-bred pig the farmer hadn't got round to mentioning to t'Ministry and thereby adding to the blizzard of paperwork.

The War-Ag operated Fordson tractors that had spikes on their rear wheels for gripping the land. Ouch! When such a tractor was being moved from one farm to another, it should have been fitted with metal bands to protect the road. The driver did not always bother to do this. A Fordson was the first tractor that many a Dales farmer had seen. It was just a tractor, designed to pull something. What it pulled tended to rive up or block old field drains. The tractor also left dollops of muck in t'farmyard.

The corn that was sown in what were traditionally meadows grew well enough. When it was as high as a Swaledale tup's eye, the Good Lord (who was, of course, a Methodist) tried the patience of the dalesfolk by sending rain to flatten the crop. This was most conspicuous where the ploughs had worked in a bony area and there was not much depth of soil.

City-bred lasses who joined the Land Army varied in their response to life in the Dales. They had their special quarters at the edge of town and were taken out to the farms by day. Many of them grew to respect the Dales farmers' wives who were, in effect, full-time, unpaid, underappreciated Land Girls. The average wife would clamber out of bed on a chilly winter's morning and rouse the fire, which had been carefully "banked up" with small coal or peat on the previous evening. She'd put

Continued on page 73.

Above: "Don't smile!" A wedding party at Settle during the 1914-18 war had fixed expressions during the long photographic exposure.

Left: Farm children, the girls having well-laundered smocks as worn at school.

Above: Goose-plucker and tea-drinkers at Israel, on the moorside near Clapham.

Above, right: A Swaledale farmer uses a four-legged stock when clipping a Swaledale yow.

Right: Goose fair at Settle. Birds that were to be taken long distances by road usually had their webbed feet reinforced for the journey by being driven through a pool of tar.

Above: George Truelove, one of the last of the old-time rural grocers, presided over a shop at Austwick which was virtually unchanged for the fifty years he officiated behind the counter.

Left: John Kilburn, of the Hill Inn, Chapel-le-Dale, one of the last of the innkeepers who were also farmers. Among his guests was Lord Tweedsmuir, better-known as the writer John Buchan.

Above: A competitor in the annual Three Peaks Cyclo-Cross.
Below: Two horses being used to haul a car, which had been engaged in a motor trial up the awesome Park Rash, near Kettlewell.

Farmer Cloughton, of Sedbusk, watches as a young dalesman contrives to cross all joints and include plenty of "throughs" when gap-walling.

Left: Another study of the Sedbusk farmer, who is holding a Swaledale sheep, usually referred to as a Swardle.

Bottom, left: Bob Preston, photographed at Sannet Hall near Stainforth.

Below: Elizabeth Middleton, of Dent, who with Mrs Betty Hartley demonstrates the ancient local craft of hand-knitting.

Above: An early Pennine bus has skidded to a halt in snow near Ingleton.

Below: The Wensleydale bus, operated by United.

Two Dales personalities. *Above:* Alf Wight, better-known as James Herriot, the vet. *Below:* Hannah Hauxwell, a television star, has a ride on an all-terrain vehicle with Chris Alderson whose sheep graze big pastures at Aisgill.

the kettle on the hob for the first cuppa of the day, then rouse her sons, who of course must be fortified by hot tea before venturing outdoors. A can of tea was taken into the shippon for dad, who had slipped out to work without anyone noticing.

Breakfast consisted of a pan of porridge and a fry-up of a dozen rashers of fatty bacon. The porridge was warmed up at the fire and the bacon on a frying pan that rested on a paraffin stove. Every dalehead farm reeked of paraffin. Then the lile woman around whom the farm life revolved would set about washing up the breakfast things, plus the utensils and buckets used for hand-milking the dozen cows. And her long day was only just beginning…

What did the Dales farmers think of the Land Girls who toured the area ploughing, discing, seeding and threshing? One farmer who had first thought of them as "nobbut lile lasses in pants" lived to applaud them for the pride they took in their work. They were not as rough with the machines as the men.

Some Land Girls would stay in the Dales – as housewives and the mothers of another generation of dalesfolk. A Wensleydale lad who was making slow progress with the Land Girl at his farm took her for a walk. They saw a sheep licking the face of another sheep. Said the shy lad, seeing a chance of stating his intentions: "I could do that."She replied: "Go ahead. They're your sheep."

Look, Duck and Vanish

THE LOCAL Defence Volunteers, LDV for short, were known to local wiseacres as "Look, Duck and Vanish." Dignity was assumed when they were provided with uniforms and re-named the Home Guard. Now they exchanged their pitchforks for weapons, demonstrating their skills to their relatives and friends at local galas. Slightly more glamorous in the eyes of young ladies in the Craven district, where the RAF had large dumps of bombs awaiting delivery to the airfields, were the "men in blue," widely known as the Brylcream Boys.

A contingent of the Home Guard was charged with defending Ribblehead railway viaduct, in case some enemy paratroops dropped in for more than a chat. If such was part of the German war plan, the invaders would have encountered several chilled part-time soldiers with one gun between them. They took their job seriously, for the viaduct – a giant structure in dark limestone extending across the dalehead towards Blea Moor – carried rail traffic that was important to the war effort.

After a term of duty, the part-time soldiers returned to Ribblehead station, where customarily they checked the ammunition. One man insisted that he had removed the bullet from the rifle. To illustrate the point, he pulled the trigger. There was an explosion, a whiff of acrid fumes and a neat hole appeared in the ceiling of the station waiting room.

At a cottage on Kisdon, Upper Swaledale, the Home Guard maintained look-outs at night. One of them heard an aero engine with a wavering sound. This was usually taken to mean an enemy aircraft. A bomb was dropped on Stainmore. It was said the Germans were trying to demolish the railway viaduct. A gamekeeper named Tom Wilson presided over the local Home Guard. If a plane crashed, he was one of the first on the scene. A pilot jabbered so much, the dalesmen could not make out what he was saying. They thought he was talking in German but turned out to be "one of ours."

Then there was the Battle of Hellifield. It might be said to have begun when Colonel Clay of Airton and his adjutant, Major J E E Yorke of Halton Place, received a message from the police inspector at Settle asking them to call urgently. He then produced a map that had been found in a bus at Burnley. The map showed the whole of the Craven area, as far as Oughtershaw. Various farms were underlined and the words "Friends here" were written beside them.

It was deduced that Hellifield railway station was to be taken over by an Irish army commanded by a German captain. The police inspector wanted a guard composed of the Home Guard to be at Hellifield on the night when an invasion was expected. No one stopped to wonder how the Irish Army would arrive. The last passenger train would have gone and the sight of hundreds of parachuters descending like dandelion seeds from a night sky was bound to be noticed.

The police inspector mustered a force of 40 of his own men. Major Yorke borrowed an old Sunbeam van from Walter Oliphant, the local garage proprietor, and drove to Wakefield to collect 30 rifles and about 200 rounds of .303 ammunition. The police moved into the railway station and the Home Guard formed a Thin Khaki Line at the periphery, holding rifles which, when unpacked, were found to be covered with grease that had been smeared on them in 1918. A password was chosen. It would be "Salmon." To the Home Guard officers, the manoeuvre was akin to that employed on the grouse moors and, of course, they chose to occupy the equivalent of the best butt. Bottles of beer and whisky clanked in each pocket.

The police inspector had not given his men the password, so that when two policemen with revolvers walked down the railway line they were startled to hear the cries of "Salmon! Salmon!" When Home Guard rifles were levelled at their heads, it was the turn of the police to be shocked.

Major Yorke decided to walk to the village and report that the police had not been given the password. As he reached the entrance to the tunnel leading to the platforms, he heard sounds of a terrific row and saw a policeman with one hand up and the other clasping a pistol. Levelling a rifle at him was the Vicar of Gisburn, who was shouting: "Salmon, salmon, salmon!"

The Home Guard manned their posts until dawn. Nothing unusual occurred and boredom set in. When a gunshot was heard from the station, everyone rallied, stood up and rattled the bolts of their rifles. Nothing else happened and it turned out that a man who was lucky to have some ammunition had pressed the trigger of his rifle by mistake.

The guard over Hellifield station was mounted for about a month. No one solved the mystery of the map found on the bus at Burnley. Was it genuine or an imaginative hoax? The Battle of Hellifield ended with only one shot being fired.

A Load o' Good Muck

GOOD MUCK was the most valuable free gift to the Dales farmer. A liberal coating of muck put fresh heart into jaded land. A farmer was not joking when, having visited his doctor, and being told the extent of the professional fee, began slowly to peel banknotes off a roll taken from his back pocket. The doctor, a busy man, said: "It will be easier if you give me a cheque." Said the farmer: "Cheque be blowed. Thou's going down in my accounts as 'three loads o' muck'."

A dalesman who was visiting relatives in Bradford passed a hall as a crowd of Methodist parsons who were attending a conference left for a lunch break. Said the man from the Dales: "I reckon parsons is like good muck – best spread out." The aged man lying on his death bed was asked by a visitor to look around when he got to Heaven and if he met "Our Fred" to tell him he had bought Sykes's Meadow. The poorly man said: "Does ta think that if I get to Heaven I'll have time to go clomping about looking for thy Fred. Onnyroad, if I do see him, I'll tell him t'meadow will bide a bit o' good muck."

Throughout the winter, the farmer and his men were in part lavatory attendants. While foddering the young cattle and milking t'milk beasts, there was the inevitable *plop, plop* as bovine bowels were cleared. In March, when the ground was likely to be firm and the season not yet "growy," the muck was transferred from the midden-steads to the fields.

One man and his horse and cart could run many a small farm high up the Dales. An outbarn was set so that it was handy to the meadow-land. The cart was loaded up and neat heaps of muck left on the land. When the heaps had weathered a day or two, and t'fire had gone out of them, they were scaled [spread] using a fork. The smell hung about the field and the farmhouse for days on end. Sometimes, it was so strong, you might taste it.

By early summer, the "herby" meadows were multi-coloured with flowering plants. An application of muck also fed thistles by the hundred. Stubbing them in the pastures was a languid job in sunny weather. The big Scotch thistles almost needed a cross-cut to fell them. By the time a man had worked across a field, the sun had wilted the thistles and cows, following up, dined greedily on them.

The tale is told in Wharfedale of a young farmer who had it in mind to buy a field and wanted a second opinion. He asked his father to accompany him to the land. The father was blind but the son quietly insisted he should be present. They rode their horses into the field. Father said: "Tie my hoss to a thistle." The lad, looking around, said: "I can't see a thistle." Said the father: "Let's go, lad. The land's no good if it wean't grow thistles."

Church and Chapel

IN AREAS where the disciples of John Wesley were numerically strong, there was a Sabbath hush of such intensity that even the sheep were disinclined to bleat. Icy stares were directed towards any child seen walking towards the toy cupboard.

Churchfolk might relax in their observance of the Lord's Day but Chapelfolk scarcely raised their voices above a whisper till Chapel-time. Then, at a village chapel, the appointed preacher would mount the rostrum-like pulpit and announce the first hymn, which was usually a rouser. Anyone within a quarter of a mile of t'chapil would realise, from the uprush of sound, why the building had been provided with a high-pointed roof.

The supporters of Church (Anglican) and Chapel (mostly Methodist) formed two distinct groups. Methodists were inclined to think of church as being dull and repetitive. To most Anglicans, Methodists got het-up [were over-emotional] and the prayers of a local preacher were most certainly repetitive and clique-ridden, especially "We thank thee, heavenly father..." Even the Almighty must have been tired of being thanked in such a torrent of words.

The great days of Nonconformity were in the past, when a joyful brother might kick out the back of the pew in front of him. A Grassington woman, intensely moved during a mission, shouted: "O Lord, tak our Jack and 'od him ower Hell's fire wi' his boots." Then, realising they were new boots, she added: "But nobbut give him a swither."

In the dales, gentry were thinly spread and inclined to go to Church. Most of the farming community and ordinary working class folk in villages were Chapel. An Anglican vicar tended to be undemanding, one man commending himself to his congregation by taking up a collection monthly. Methodism benefited from being run by local folk, with periodic visits from the minister.

The parish churches of the Dales varied in size and style, from huge places of worship like that at Kirkby Malham to modest chapels-of-ease

with seating for no more than fifty people. Some churches looked old, with their castellated towers, their lead roofs, grinning gargoyles and memorials to generations of notable families. Many had been restored, and their character ruined, by the Victorians.

A visiting bishop, alarmed when he saw a shrub growing from the tower of a Dales church, mentioned it to one of the churchwardens, who was glad the visitor had noticed it. He added: "You should see it in spring when it's flowering."

A Dales vicar was as plain as the people. One who was about to retire after lengthy service was told by parishioners of the accomplishments of t'new chap. He read his Bible in Greek. The old man retorted: "English was good enough for St Paul and it's good enough for me."

Methodists were generally plain folk who hated frills, such as parsons wearing gowns, crosses on communion tables and sermons that were lah-de-dah. A good service was mainly extempore. The local preacher, yan of us, spoke as the spirit moved him and had some homely remarks with references to local people. The almost operatic fervour of some Methodist services was fearful to small children. One preacher who was noisy and demonstrative in the pulpit so alarmed a boy that he tugged on Granny's sleeve and said, tremblingly: "What would happen if he got out?"

In days of big families, it didn't take much to pack a place. At a moorside chapel near Clapham, at the beginning of what some folk called t'Bible Belt, the place would be packed and preachers raised their voices till the rafters rang. They took off their jackets and brayed t'pulpit to drive home what they considered important points of discussion. A preacher like Richard Alderson, of Grisedale, was so intense in his religion he was almost a mystic.

Some preachers had morbid themes and a choice of what one organist described as "death hymns." There were grave warnings in the sermon of Judgement and the Life to Come. Preachers in Swaledale "laid down the law, I'll tell you. They varra near freetened you to deearth." Others were less effective. His ailing wife asked a man who returned from chapel about the service. He was a taciturn man. There were long pauses. Who had preached? Mr Smith. What had he preached about? Sin. What did he say about it? The man gave a deep sigh and remarked: "He was agin it!"

The class system was nothing to do with status but with a group within a group, which met on a weekday under a leader for Bible study, prayer and discussion. A newcomer said to the Class Leader: "Some folk say I', cracked." There was a surprising response from the Class Leader, who said: "Let us pray....Oh, Lord, crack a few more people; there's plenty of work for 'em down here." At a chapel where a prayer meeting was held after the Sunday evening service, two old men thumped and banged cushions, raising clouds of dust, in their fervent approach to Christianity.

At revival meetings, new converts were sought. They'd get hold of people and drag them out of the pews. It was quite an ordeal. The organist, being "fastened to t'organ," usually escaped. Damascus Road-type conversions were known. A testifer would say: "I were coming down t'paddock amang t'tewits [lapwings] and was a gay seet [untidy]. I was carrying a calf bucket. When I saw a bright light in t'sky, I were that capped, I dropped t'bucket, got down on my knees and prayed."

Methodists had a special aversion to drink, which to them was "the Devil in suspension." A noted abstainer was taking a service when he arranged two drinking glasses and a matchbox on the pulpit. He announced that one glass contained some whisky, the other held water, and in the matchbox were two worms. One worm was dropped in the whisky where, he reported, it writhed then died. The other worm settled languidly in the water. "Now friends," said the preacher, "what does that prove?" A farmer rose stiffly to his feet and said: "If tha's got worms, drink whisky."

Children were enrolled in the Young Abstainers or Band of Hope before they had given up gripe-water. They were taught to sing:

> *My drink is water bright, water bright,*
> *Water bright;*
> *My drink is water bright, from the*
> *Crystal spring.*

A minister greeted a toper who, on Sunday evening, unexpectedly turned up in the back pew of a village chapel. Said the minister: "It was good to see you in chapel last evening." The toper remarked: "Oh, that's where I got to. I mun tell t'wife."

Black Markets

WARTIME restrictions were intended to control the flow of food from the farms to the populace. At the auction mart, a panel of graders estimated the weight and condition of sheep. The government paid the producer accordingly. Notice had to be given of the stock that would be presented and there were, for a time, no auction fees, nor any "luck," usually a silver corn handed to the purchase on completion of a deal.

Feeding stuffs for cattle were exchangeable for cash plus coupons. None of the coupons was wasted, for if a farmer had a surplus he usually sold the tokens at £5 each, which was good money in those days. People hankered for extra food. The dreams of urban folk, living in their stone-and-concrete jungles, were mainly of sinking teeth into lumps of lean meat. The domestic pig, the humble bunny and any aged hens were slaughtered for the family and, in some cases, for the Black Market.

When I was at the *Craven Herald* in the early years of the war, a parcel arrived for the advertisement manager. The parcel had been torn here and there and sprouted feathers. White feathers. Not the symbol of cowardice but a present – a "lile bit o' summat" – from a farmer friend up t'Dales. In exchange, the advert manager had helped the farmer with his books.

The advert manager snipped the string that held the parcel together. What would it be this time? It was undoubtedly a bird – a change from the usual bit of ham or bit o' pork or even, at pig-killing time, some nourishing sausages. It was none of these things. From the corpse within the packet marched battalions of red mites. A letter from Sam Stables, our Grassington correspondent, referred to the albino carrion crow he had several times reported as being in Wharfedale. The reports had not been used. Now he offered the bird itself as proof.

Pig-killing was one of the great days in the calendar of a farming family. A pig was slain when there was an "r" in the month. In Dentdale, "they worked it among themselves so there'd be one killing every week-end. Even the blood was 'catched' and used for puddings." The farmer's wife boiled the pig's feet, another delicacy. As much as 20 lb of really good lard could be obtained from a well-fed pig when it was rendered down.

Before the war, people turned up to share in the feasting. Since the war, all such animals had to be reported and the principal of food rationing applied. Not a few pigs died in seclusion and the meat was kept away from prying eyes.

At an inn much favoured by police offers, hams were kept "under the slates," suspended from six-inch nails that were driven into the beams. Hams with weights ranging from 10 lb to 35 lb were kept here. At one time, the beams creaked under the weight of seventeen hams. For the sum of 5s, a diner received, in the depths of war, a bountiful meal of ham and eggs, sherry trifle, buttered scones and tea. Two frying pans were in almost constant use. One was for ham and the other for eggs, eight or nine at a time, the pan resting on part of an open fire.

At the Sportsmen's Inn, in the upper valley of the Dee, "mine host" had developed an interest in art for above the fireplace in his private lounge was hung a rather lurid water-colour. Those in the know were not the least interested in the picture; they waited until it was taken down, revealing a cavity containing his special wartime food store.

Disposing of a dead pig called for much careful planning. A Malhamdale farmer loaded meat into the back of an old van and set off for town. En route, he saw a police cordon but he kept his foot down on the accelerator. Those manning the cordon had to scatter. The farmer's wife said: "Tha's done it now. They'll have got thi registration number." He replied: "They won't. Just before I set off, I covered it with cow-muck."

A signalman on the Settle-Carlisle railway supplied large quantities of food, mainly rabbits and eggs, to folk living in the Leeds area. He tied a dead rabbit to the railing in front of the box to indicate that rabbits were available. The fireman of a goods train would leap off the footplate when the train had come almost to a halt. He sprinted up the steps of the signal box, grabbed some rabbits, paid for them at the rate of half-a-crown a couple and returned to the still-moving train. A Leeds driver who saw the gibbeted rabbit too late is said to have applied the brakes and reversed a few hundred yards to collect a supply.

A Wensleydale farmer who saw a food inspector crossing the yard on his way to the door of the farmhouse had to think quickly to escape detection, for there was a good supply of illicit pig meat in the place. He told his wife to slip into bed and then place pork on either side of her. The inspector paid only a brief visit to the bedroom, with its pale-looking woman who looked half-dead. Later, when the inspector was well clear of the farm, she said to her husband: "Next time, you'll go to bed. I've never bin so cold in my life as I was when I ligged aside all that pig meat."

With the 1939-45 war over, food rationing continued. Indeed, 1947, with its fearful blizzards, saw the Dales communities reduced to the edge of starvation. The Ministry of Food officials raided an auction mart and found a few hams that the owners had intended to sell at 5s a lb.

When subsidies for agriculture were announced, it was the end of the Dales farmer's finely-tuned independence. Subsidies set a wrong value on cost and prices. They put farmers at the mercy of a government that rarely got its sums right and might soon demand a drastic reduction in public spending on agriculture.

Flowers of many varieties scent the air. The whole is a prodigious example of giving, the generosity of nature and of man.

Doreen Cripps at Parcevall Hall.

1950-59

Machines took the place of casual labourers. The farm man now had a cotter pin instead of a wisp of straw in his mouth. The tractor was common-place and in a breathless decade the baling machine arrived, ingesting rows of hay and regurgitating them as compact bales. In winter, the twine cut from the bales was the Dales farmer's best friend, being used to fettle [repair] or fasten gates and, in emergency, to act as galluses [braces]. At Gunnerside Lodge, in Swaledale, grouse-shooters kept up the old style by turning up for grouse-shooting in Daimlers and Rolls Royces. Many a small-time farmer forsook bike or bus for a car. One man took his new car back to the garage and said: "It's not rattlin' reight."

A Dalesman's Diary

I BECAME a freeman of the Dales, being welcomed everywhere as an emissary of *The Dalesman* magazine. An invitation to "come in, lad – have a cup o' tea" was invariably attended by a full-blown meal, with apologies that there was "nowt warm." There were gentle reminders, as the price per issue gradually climbed, that when the magazine was first published, in April, 1939, it cost thruppence.

Holiday visitors were confined to a season that began at Easter, flopped till Whitunstide and ended in October. Campers were rare, giving special point to a comment recorded by Ella Pontefract. A farmer looked at a camper's tent and said: "Tha's nivver gaen to lig under yon' lump o' clout."

Caravans had been vastly improved from the 1920s, when many were fashioned using tapestry lined interiors and with an outer skin formed of a soft material that preceded hardboard. Gilbert Kilburn, of Cara Cars, Ilkley, related when cows ate five panels during the night when a caravan was standing at Appletreewick, in Wharfedale. Gilbert provided Ella Pontefract and Marie Hartley with a caravan used as a base for the Dales journeys described in several books.

Like Misses Pontefract and Hartley, I looked for characters – for individuals, native-born, with minds of their own. They had quaint speech and whimsical manners. Dales speech was spiced with dialect. A finnicky woman was said to "leuk for lice i' bald 'eeards." Folk speech was in clear contrast with "wireless talk" which, by implication, was posh. When it was suggested to an old chap he might replace his battered old radio, he said: "Nay – I've just getten used to t'folk on this 'un."

My Dales Diary filled with notes, such as the experience of Derek Thompson, librarian of the first mobile library to tour the West Riding dales, who set off walking, with a pile of books, from the parked library van to the back door of a remote farmhouse. As he neared the door, a dog approached him with bared fangs. Then another dog appeared, grabbed the first animal by an ear and held it down until the librarian reached safety.

My first editorial encounter for *The Dalesman* was with Old Mick, the bull walloper. This Irishman knew of the Yorkshire reputation for "tightness wi' brass" but found a generous attitude towards him when he arrived in North Ribblesdale just after the Great War. Now, some thirty years later, I tracked him down for a chat and to test the theory that Mick could drink twelve pints of ale to twelve strokes of the clock.

Mick had a wartime injury to his throat. It was said to have been caused when an enemy bayonet lacerated his "Adam's apple," which meant he could no longer gulp. Any liquid he imbibed went down as fast as gravity permitted. He never came near drinking the 12 pints before the clock signified noon, but most days someone tested the theory and Mick was happy to oblige. So my first expense sheet at *The Dalesman* concerned a supply of "strong drink."

Mick told me he had been a big drinker all his life. His father drank a fortune before "finding it out" and preaching temperance. Mick did not regret what he had spent on beer though he chanted:

In pub, spent sub., and spent it with good cheer;
Now I'm going down the road, saying damn and blast the beer.

Mick was a drover. He would have been daft if he had lived up to his nickname and had walloped a bull. His droving days were over, though as he plodded along the roads around Settle he carried a privet stick, the successor to the real emblem of his occupation, which was a hazel switch.

George Metcalfe, a retired roadman I met in Appersett told me he had worked in Aysgarth parish for thirty-eight years, travelling twenty-two miles a day by push bike for 18s a week. He owned the first bicycle in Appersett – and couldn't ride it! Money being scarce, he had acquired it in exchange for some poultry. When I first met George he was sitting by the bridge, clay pipe in mouth, old cap high on the back of his head and well down to his eyes. His high cheeks bristled with grey hairs that eventually merged with a bushy moustache. He re-charged his clay pipe, remarking: "You can't tell whether a pipe is wood or clay when you've smoked it a bit." I inquired about his health. He said: "I've got to t'stage in life when I'm just wearing mi clothes up."

Thomas White, who worked at one of the Dales quarries, was known to his friends as Old Gen. He had wielded a shovel for fifty years, commenting: "I've always had a shovel in my hand. Nowadays it's all pressin' buttons and riding up and down." I asked him if he had any funny tales to relate. He replied: "There's nowt funny about shops like this…" Was he thinking of retirement? He replied, reflectively: "I've bin thinking about it." What would he do with himself if he retired? "There's nowt here, 'cept drinking." How much had beer cost him fifty years before? "Thruppence a pint – an' I managed four or five pints a night." What did he manage nowadays? He chuckled and said: "Oh, summat about t'same."

Gilbert Brown, of Malham, would have been unhappy in a crowd. He had some good chapel tales, such as that of a farm man who put a half sovereign in the collection plate instead of sixpence. Afterwards, he approached the steward and asked for the return of the gold coin. The steward said: "If tha taks it back, tha'll be damned." The farm man said: "If I don't take it back, I'll be beggered."

Rural Buses

BY 1950, what for a few years had been the great rural bus service was showing signs of decline as cars became commonplace. Yet each bus still retained a conductor, most frequently a woman. At busy times, half a dozen passengers would be standing. Once, on a snow-streaked Buckhaw Brow, passengers in the local bus clambered out to give it a push on the last steep stretch. In another area, during a wet (and muddy) spell, someone had scrawled on the side of a dirt-streaked bus: "Don't wash me – plant summat."

Bus-wise, the great day of the week was market day. All the world and its parcels crowded on to the morning bus, to return in the early evening with still more parcels. Even if a passenger had no packages of his own, there would be plenty of other people's to share. It might be a piece of ironmongery or a basket of groceries. There might be a couple of live hens or even – as I once experienced – a goat, which was taken to the back of the bus and did not disgrace itself, though some passengers complained of the smell.

In the heyday of rural buses, a bull calf lapped in sacking, beginning a journey to t'auction mart, exercised a powerful pair of lungs. Perhaps it was complaining about the smokers. The air in the bus was heavy with the fumes of tobacco. Nobody in their right mind would open a window, if indeed they could be opened. Rust was an effective adhesive.

A driver on one Dales service wore a long white coat in summer and a blue overcoat in winter. He was also the conductor, giving tickets only for return journeys. He never had time to bother with singles. Folk paid and he simply pushed the money into the bag. When a bus was scrapped, a partition near to the driver's seat was ripped out, revealing a considerable number of coins that had slipped behind it.

The first bus service in Swaledale, about 1920, was maintained by an old flat-bodied Seabrook lorry on which 25 seats, in rows, were fitted. The seats came from a four-in-hand horse bus. The bus was owned by Dick Guy, who was fond of recalling that the passengers sat in the open and had a bumpy journey for the wheels were shod with solid rubber tyres.

This Swaledale service operated only on the day of the week when Richmond held its market. Subsequently, the Percival Brothers ran a bus service, initially in competition with a bus owned by Tim Scatchard, who kept the Black Bull in Reeth. There was much racing up and down the dale road to secure passengers. Eventually, Tim Scatchard withdrew from the route.

The Skipton-Buckden bus service was extended in summer over Kidstones Pass into Wensleydale. A driver, miles from anywhere, stopped the bus when he encountered a bull in the middle of the road. The bull walked up to the (red) bus and sniffed it over. Then it backed a few lengths – and charged. Both headlamps were shattered.

A conductor on a bus travelling between Grassington and Ilkley was stranded at Appletreewick. As the bus was driven up the steep main street, he told the driver he had a parcel to deliver to the post office. "Don't bother stopping; just slow down and I'll drop off," he added. The parcel was delivered and the conductor tramped to the hilltop, discovering that the bus had gone without him. He thumbed a lift in a van and caught up the bus at Barden. On another day, the bus arrived at Barden with five minutes to spare. The driver and conductor nodded off and slept so soundly that neither of them awoke until after the time the bus should have been in Ilkley, about eight miles away.

The blue-painted buses of the Aldersons operated between Settle and Horton-in-Ribblesdale. In the days when, after heavy rain, the river spread over the road near Studfold, it was not unknown for passengers to retract their legs. George Lund, of Stainforth, entered the bus wearing a back-can that was normally used for milk but put into service on market day as a receptacle for over-ripe fruit and unwanted fish, which he bore triumphantly home and fed to his hens.

Orange-painted Pennine buses were to be seen on the road from Skipton to Malham and from Skipton to Ingleton with (for a time) a service through to Lancaster. In the pioneering days of the 1920s, a bus had 14 seats. A policeman who boarded a bus at Long Preston after dark had been told the bus was full but was permitted to travel. It was a real crush with 40 people competing for the few seats. When the bus stopped at Hellifield, some of the men who had been travelling on the running board in the dark came round to pay their fares. The policeman asked the driver, Harry Fletcher, where they had been riding. Said Harry, quick-wittedly: "They haven't been riding; they've been running at t'back."

Is Ta Courtin'?

KISSING and cuddling in public were considered to be "soft." In an area of far-flung farms and hamlets, love always found a way. If a girl lived three or four miles from her young man it was not surprising that he courted but once a week. Up at Tan Hill, Susan Peacock helped a lovelorn dalesman with his courting by writing letters on his behalf. It went on for years. In the end, the couple married.

With no formal sex education at school and just "mucky talk" in the playground, it surprised no one that many a courtship ended abruptly with the discovery there was a child on the way. A sixteen-year-old who had little experience of men was told by her Grannie not to trust a man of any age. She added: "A chap who can drag an empty sack can get a child."

Otherwise, the long courtship was common. A man who had been "walking out" with a lady for fourteen years said: "Isn't it time we got wed?" She replied: "Aye, lad – but who'd have us?" On the farms, there was a close season for courting at lambing time or haytime.

KISSING GATE.

Before the Young Farmers' Clubs mixed up rural youth, many a liaison was established after a chapel service when, in the populous areas, droves of lasses and lads set off along t'road, walking t'full width. "First yan would click, and he'd tak her off, then somebody 'ud click wi' annuder. It went on till it got down to one or two 'at nobody wanted."

In a Dales market town, courting sometimes involved a Sunday afternoon walk through the local cemetery, where the lad – if he had a Dales pedigree – was keen to show off the graves of kith and ken as evidence of the family's dependability. One lad went too far when he said: "Here's where Grandad and Gran were buried," then "Here's where Mum and Dad were buried," then "And over here is where I'd like us to be buried."

A lad from Lunds, near the source of the Ure, courted a lass from Cam Houses, near the source of the Wharfe. A Wensleydale lad was fond of a girl in Swaledale. He had to cross Buttertubs Pass by pushbike, often in terrible weather. At a North Craven house, a widowed mother looked forward to her daughter's courting night, dressing for the occasion. She sat in the same room as her daughter and an older suitor, who was a joiner. One night, he was so bored he tipped over the sofa and carried out a long-awaited repair.

Some young people became acquainted at Dales dances. If you had t'last dance with a girl, you took her home. You were wet through many a time. One lad who danced with a lass and discovered she lived at Thorney Mire, one and a-half miles from the dance hall, persuaded a friend with a lantern to go with them.

A lad who was accepted by a girl for the last waltz usually asked if he could see her home. So it was that a lile lad and a somewhat plump lass had the last dance and she agreed to be walked home, warning the lad that she lived three miles from the dance hall. After a mile, he asked if he could have a kiss. She agreed. He was so small he could not reach her lips, so he espied a milk kit at the side of the road, slurred it into position, climbed on it and had his kiss. The walk continued. After another mile, he requested another kiss. Said the girl: "No – one time out, one kiss." The lad sighed and remarked: "Then I'd better get rid of this milk kit."

Dales Weddings

JAMES HERRIOT, the best-known vet in the Dales, was married at the picturesque Wensley Church for a BBC series based on books written by Alf Wight. In reality, Alf married Joan at Thirsk, where the veterinary practice was based. It was a November day in the early austere days of the 1939-45 war. Three other people were present at the ceremony. Canon Young was the clergyman. Fred Rymer gave the bride away and Donald Sinclair – the Seigfried Farnon of the James Herriot books – was the best man.

Alf and his bride, who became the Helen of the books, had scarcely a penny in the world, beyond a wedding gift of £5 from Donald. They went to the cinema at Richmond before heading into Wensleydale on a working honeymoon, for they spent much of the time tuberculin-testing cattle.

In the Dales, news quickly spread that "so-and-so's putten t'assings [banns] in." Those were the days when no one had the cheek to send out a list of requirements as wedding gifts. You accepted what was offered.

There was inevitably a hideous purple vase or some other decorative object that the bridal couple immediately decided would be hidden except on the days when the donor came for tea.

The mother of a bride said: "Our Lizzie's getten a new house. Lots of good furniture. And a car." Her friend asked: "What about her husband?" Mother replied: "She can't stand him. But there's allus summat, isn't there?"

Some young dalesfolk had to get married, preferably before any sexual indiscretion began to show. "It was maybe a good job in some cases or they wouldn't hev been wed." A middle-aged bridegroom in Wharfedale confessed to his best man, as they stood at the front of the church on the wedding day, that he was having second thoughts about his bride-to-be. The best man whispered: "Serves thi reight. Tha's bin round t'orchard and finished up wi' a crab apple."

The success of Dales farming depended largely on the men taking brides from the local community – women attuned to life in remoter places and to the relentless work on a farm. To marry a lass out of t'town was also courting trouble. A widow, who had a farm at the dalehead, lost her daughter to a "town lad." Eventually, when they had a baby, she was invited to town for the week-end. She left her primitive little farm, with its flagged floor, its stone slopstone and pump in the yard, for a new Council house with all mod-cons. When a tour of the house was completed, the young couple and the baby waited in the hallway for her comments. She said: "Place is all reight. But how's ta going to get t'coffin down yon stairs?"

In lile churches and chapels, the *Wedding March* was wheezed out via a harmonium. A marriage-hardened man suggested the hymns might include *Fight the Good Fight*. Convention was met with *O Perfect Love* and *Love Divine*. A vicar was surprised when, on asking the bridegroom if he would take this woman to be thy lawful wife, heard him say: "I come o' purpose."

On the wedding day, in years long ago, tying up the church gates ensured a supply of small change for the children. In Coverdale, some mischievous lads heated up coins before tossing them into the street.

Those who scrambled for them had to mount guard on individual coins while they cooled. The bride ensured good luck by throwing a cracked plate over one shoulder. Rice was thrown before confetti became popular. At Bainbridge, the bridal car was held up when two men stood with a ladder between them and the road remained blocked until the bridegroom had handed over a small amount of cash.

Receptions, especially in chapel families, were sedate affairs. A farmer who was seeing the youngest of five children to the altar was not expected to speak. Then, rising to his feet at the appropriate time, he remarked: "Last Wednesday, when I went to Skipton Auction, an old friend came up me and said: 'I hear tell thou's getting' selt up o' Saturday'." A stern Methodist uncle insisted that at the wedding of his nephew the drink supplied at the reception should be no stronger than lemonade.

A thrifty farmer, told the reception must be held at a local inn, went along to negotiate a price per head for the food. After an hour, he had succeeded in reducing the price almost to a give-away level. He then said, triumphantly: "How much would it be if I fetched my own ham?"

Many couples couldn't afford a honeymoon. Others went to relatives or friends who had migrated from the Dales to the North East towns or the textile belt of East Lancashire. Jim Smith hired a horse and cart from Elijah Allen of Hawes and went round Aysgarth Falls and back. By the 1950s, there was even talk of some couples going abroad.

Cuckoo Town

A USTWICK is so called because it lies "east of Clapham." It is also known as Cuckoo Town from one of the daft tales told about a village that straggles along the edge of the limestone country. Local men had an idea that if they prevented the cuckoo from returning to Africa there would be perpetually good weather in the area. So, noticing a bird roosting in a tree, they built a wall round it. Next morning, the bird escaped by flying over the top.

Austwick folk had only one knife. It was of the short variety, used by a butcher and known as a whittle. When not in use, the knife was hanging from one of the big trees near the church. If someone wished to use it, and it had not been returned, they toured the village shouting "whittle to t'tree."

It is also related that an Austwick man visiting the doctor at Settle left his surgery in a rainstorm. So the doctor loaned him a furled umbrella. It was the first the visitor had seen. Arriving back home, he wondered how he might preserve it until he returned to Settle on the following market day. The "humbrel," as he called it, was too large to go through a window or even a door, so he tied it up in one of the outbuildings. When he made the return journey to Settle, proudly holding up the umbrella, it was a gloriously sunny day.

Other daft tales are told and no one in Austwick seemed to be upset by them. Compared with Clapham, a village owned by Ingleborough Estate, Austwick was a village of freeholders, where folk spoke their mind. Clapham was at the mouth of Clapdale and swaddled in trees. Austwickers lived in an open setting, with a backdrop provided by three little peaks. Norber was the north hill. Moughton was flat-topped and floriferous, and Oxenber was lightly draped by trees because of an ancient rule that the only timber to be collected was that which had fallen naturally.

Characters proliferated. Jimmy-Johnny were, indeed, two farming brothers. At the time we lived in Austwick, they had some land behind our home, which is known by the down-to-earth name of Spouts Croft. Johnny (or could it have been Jimmy?) preferred travel by pony and trap and, when he brought the outfit to a halt in the field behind our cottage and surveyed his prize cattle, he might have been a Roman centurion reviewing his troops. The brothers were fond of trotting horses and for a time it was possible to see spindly-legged trotters pulling carts laden with hay.

Christabella Ingilby, a member of the family who had lived in fine state at Harden, was now subsisting in what had been a gardener's cottage but retained the regality of minor royalty. She was also a thoroughly charming person who persuaded half the village to bestride the stage of the Parish Hall and the other half to occupy seats watching them as they presented yet another of Mr Shakespeare's plays.

One had a tingling sensation along the spine on being among those attending a rehearsal, in a gloomy room, when a stray beam of light rested on a Buddha. Another ray lit up the seamed but beautiful face of Christabella as she spoke quietly of what she believed Shakespeare had in mind. No one liked to inquire how her family had come to lose its wealth. One of the tales told of this lovely lady was that when a villager who was helping with a jumble sale called and asked if she had any jumble, she replied: "I wear mine."

Chris Cheetham, naturalist extraordinary, had arrived in Austwick after a career in textiles that had not held his full attention. Chris, when young, resolved never to shave nor to wear long trousers. So he went about with a face bristling like a brush, with his knees revealed and with plimsolls on his feet. His passion was natural history. He was an authority on the local flora and whenever he took anyone into the countryside they returned in no mood for supper. Chris had repeatedly offered them tit-bits of grasses and herbs, inviting them to "taste this" or "taste that." Salad burnet had a cucumber flavour.

Chris was known to consume large quantities of fungi, observing that only one or two of the many species were poisonous. The skill was in knowing which to avoid. He had a species of daddy-longlegs named after him.

Chris never had an "infernal" combustion engine. He walked or cycled. His bike took him far and wide across Yorkshire as secretary of the Naturalists' Union. He also had a tandem on which he conveyed his mother, then over ninety years of age, for "spins" around the district. When he was not botanising, out of doors or in his home, where he spent hours peering through his microscope, he enjoyed singing with the choir in the parish church. In late life, he had an artificial hip fitted and ever afterwards complained when coming downhill that the surgeon had not left a hole through which oil could be squirted.

Nothing that happened at Austwick was ordinary. When some lads visited nearby Feizor and stripped Mr Riley's pear tree of its fruit, they returned the following night and tied the pear cores to the branches. Dave Jack did not drink tea from a cup. He used a basin, emptying into it a quarter of a pound of tea at a time and adding water until one lot of tea had lost its strength, when another was added.

The cuckoo came and went at Austwick. So did the corncrake, in the days before mechanisation and earlier haytimes destroyed its nests before it had time to rear the young. The last time this skulking brown bird, a summer visitor for nesting, was seen, a bird was being held in the mouth of a spaniel owned by the local butcher. He had been talking with a local man when the dog vanished into a meadow and collected the corncrake, which up till them had been giving its harsh repetitive call. The bird was carefully removed from the soft lips of the dog and set down in a garden. It vanished into a herbacious border – and was not seen or heard again!

What our railways require is cheaper fares and
an improved service.

KLR(1959).

1960-1969

Queen Elizabeth slept at Clapham station, where, during a tour, the Royal train was drawn up for the night. It was otherwise an unhappy time for rural railways. Dr Beeching took an axe and lopped off many of the branch lines. The Dales villages began to look smarter as the demand for rural properties by urban folk having a romantic notion of owning "a cottage in the country" boosted property prices. Best-kept village competitions had a manicuring effect on many. At Richmond, the restored Georgian Theatre was re-opened. Electricity was reaching the remoter places. One woman, accustomed to paraffin, remarked: "Doesn't it last a long time."

Dales Hostelries

THE OLD type of pub had a flagged ground floor that was liberally strewn with sawdust. Ale brought up from the cellar was served from a big jug. Men smoked, chatted, played dominoes, discussed fatstock prices, the weather and each other. In the oldest places, a spittoon stood in one corner. After a modernisation scheme, a local man said: "I miss t'spittoon." Said the landlord: "Thou allus did!"

A farm lad, entering a Dales pub, confessed: "I'm that hungry I could eat a calf." The others, ever ready to place bets, insisted that this was not possible. The farm man persisted in his claim. It was arranged that he would return in three days time and "eat a calf." But how would it be cooked and served? The barmaid suggested it should be in the form of three big pies. The farm man returned, ate one pie, then another. When the third pie was pushed towards him, he said: "Nay, lads, I can't manage that – I've got a calf to eat tonight."

Miss Peacock, who lived at Wharfe, near Austwick, told me that her father and his brother were great walkers. "When they saw a church tower, they put their best feet forward – for it was ten-to-one there was a pub beside it." Miss Peacock was unrelated to Mrs Susan Peacock, a wispy woman who, for 34 years, presided over Tan Hill Inn. She was undoubtedly the best known landlady in the Dales if only because at an elevation of 1,732 ft above sea level, the inn was "the highest licensed premises in the land."

Solitude never worried Susan, who had grown up "in quiet places." She went to Tan Hill in 1903 as the wife of Richard Parrington and mother of three daughters. Susan was twice married and died at Tan Hill in 1937. She was solitary but never lonely. Nor, with a trusty gun at hand, was she afraid of who might turn up at this remote spot.

The wind blows where it will. "There's nowt except t'pub to stop it." Once it demolished the chimney pot. At the height of the storm, Susan's husband moved round the side of the building on his hands and knees. At times, a practical joker would catch a moorland sheep and set it loose in the bar. Susan's goat was partial to chocolate. She never failed to let visitors know this and to make them aware that a supply of chocolate was available for sale.

Tan Hill was a "watering hole" for those who trudged the Pennine Way, which then was Britain's longest continuous footpath. Motorists wishing to visit Tan Hill had a choice of three routes, the most demanding being that from upper Swaledale, via West Stonesdale. The driver had to contend with two acute hairpins.

A visiting cyclist in the inter-war years recalled the joy of waking in a bedroom at the Tan Hill inn. There was the morning knock and the discovery at the door of a container of hot water for shaving. "And when you'd opened the door there was the smell of home-fed bacon being cooked. A hen or two managed to survive in the extreme conditions, so there would also be a couple of eggs for breakfast."

In the old days, the demand for ale at Tan Hill could be met by installing an 18-gallon cask per month. In winter, a cask lasted three times as long. Richard Kearton, the Swaledale gamekeeper's son who became a famous naturalist writer, noted in his biography that "eleven consecutive weeks have sometimes passed without as much as the shadow of a stranger crossing the threshold." Richard and his brother, staying at the high-lying inn, were amused when a farmer arrived and ordered a glass of ale, which loosened his tongue. He said he had been to London three times. It was a grand spot for a holiday, "but I always took care nivver to be oot after dark!"

In the 1930s, when the "wireless" was a novelty, an aura of romance lay about Tan Hill Inn. Susan had been to a Leeds studio with the Swaledale Singers. She was glad to get back to Tan Hill and remarked that t'wireless had no appeal for her. "Michael [her husband] is not struck on it either." Broadcasting made Tan Hill famous but those who ventured this way, glorying in their achievement, were relieved to find that the place was as "simple" as before.

In Dentdale, at a junction between two main streets, where cobble-stones are still in place, the George and Dragon has catered for genera-tions of visitors as well as for the local people. Years ago, a tired rambler knocked on the door. The landlady, who had a brittle temper, popped her head out of an upper winter and remonstrated with the rambler who, after a while, and having met the dragon, asked: "Could I have a word with George?"

At Hubberholme, the infant river Wharfe flows between inn and church and is spanned by a handsome bridge. Until the mid-1960s, the inn was the property of the benefice. A long established and continuing custom concerns the annual letting of the Poor Pasture, a 16-acre plot at Kirkgill that at the time of the Enclosures was purchased by a benefac-tor for the poor of the parish. After a short service in church, the incum-bent led his flock to the inn, where a goodly number of local people were already assembled. Bidding was invited and lasted until a candle placed in a saucer had burnt out.

Thousands of people got to know the grey centre passage of the Green Dragon, at Hardraw, because this was the tourist route to Hardraw Scar, from the lip of which descends a 100 ft waterfall – the highest unbroken fall in the land. At one time, Lord Wharncliffe owned the waterfall and its environs; but in 1913 his local possesions were sold. The musical festivals, with choirs and bands, still continue, though just with brass bands. Some of the bands travel big distances to attend.

The flow of water over the rim of a cliff at Hardraw is variable but unstoppable. One of the folk tales concerns a summer's day when Great Shunner Fell experienced a cloudburst. A torrent of water rose nearly half way up the walls of the lower rooms at the inn. The bridge was swept away and iron railings were bent by the force of the water. A horse in a stable opposite the inn stood belly deep in water and some pigs swam over the bottom half of the door in the same outbuilding and escaped down the fields.

Moorcock Inn, a lonely cluster of buildings on the Hawes-Sedbergh road, is mentioned on practically every map of England. At one time it was part of the large Mossdale estate owned by Kit Garnett. For years, water flowed to the inn from a large tank fed by a wind-powered pump. The Miner's Arms, on Greenhow Hill, served farmers as well as miners. The main adit of Cock Hill mine ran beneath the building. The mine prospered until the 1880s, when the pump broke down, leading to severe flooding. In the heyday of mining, the inn echoed to the chatter of the miners and the rasp of their clogs against flagstones.

Thy Pratt, the Greenhow grave-digger, suffered from a dry throat. A pint would nobbut wet one side. One day, he was so engrossed in digging a new grave he did not hear the approach of some ramblers. Thy, suddenly feeling the need for liquid refreshment, gave a great sigh and climbed from the grave. The ramblers, white-faced, scattered. When the snow-dogs howled, the licensees of the Miner's, at an elevation of 1,200 ft., might awake to find a huge drift blocking access to the inn.

Take Your Partners!

WHEN A dance was held in rooms below the old Cathole at Keld, the charge was "not aboon thruppence." Then inflation took over. The dalesfolk were attending Sixpenny Hops. At Keld, a concertina, or maybe a fiddle provided the music. It was not unknown for farmers' sons from the dale head to arrive on horseback wearing breeches and leggings. Rabbit Pie Jimmy – so called because he often sang a song about a pie – could be relied upon to sing something daft. In another room, where young men played the card game "nap," the fire would have "roasted a cow", young men played cards for hours on end.

By the 1960s, dancing vied with t'pictures in the limited leisure time. Almost every Dales village had a hall suitable for dancing, even if it was just a wooden hut of the type bought from the Army after the 1914-18 war. At Linton, in Upper Wharfedale, the structure was said to move under the surge of dancers during a Palais Glide.

Elsewhere, a slightly tilting floor brought dancers close to a white-hot stove. When a dance was about to begin at Tosside, two burly men with iron rods connected them with the stove and carried it into a corner of the car park. A middle-aged man who asked a lady to join him in a waltz eventually said: "Can you reverse?" She, looking concerned, asked: "Are you getting dizzy?" He replied: "No, lass – tha's unscrewing mi wooden leg."

A brash young lad who advanced on a farmer's daughter used an Americanism: "Say – can I borrow your frame for a shuffle?" The girl kept her "frame" to herself. At Austwick, Will Pritch emerged from the supper room at the Parish Hall. After staring at a young couple who were recuperating from food and drink, Will said: "Thou wants to git up an' shak thee supper down."

The most popular dances were those held in large villages or towns, where a band provided music and those attending dressed for the occasion. It was the Big Band period of entertainment. The annual balls organised by farming organisations offered the rural folk a respite from a wearying round of work. Farm folk converged on the hall by bus, car or bike.

Every self-respecting lad plastered his hair with Brylcream and wore a suit complete with braces and waistcoat. An unromantic aspect of that period was the style of shirt. It had a detachable collar, secured by studs. As a dancer prepared for a night hour, there would be last-minute panic because he had misplaced a collar stud. For the young lady, taffeta was the thing, even red taffeta, extending to the ankles. All had mini-handbags and silver shoes.

The vast floor was smooth – and would become smoother still after it had been sprinkled with powder and danced on for an hour or two. An orb revolving high up, against the ceiling, created a most romantic atmosphere, being composed of tiny mirrors. When a spotlight rested upon it, and the hall lights had been dimmed, the walls and ceiling were covered by a moving pattern of colourful blobs that would have put a peacock's tail to shame.

It was understood that a man would see the girl back to her chair. The territorial impulse led people to leave possessions like cardigans and jackets on their chosen seats. It would be a brave soul who took over such a seat while the tenant was dancing. When the dancers were not quick-stepping or fox-trotting to contemporary favourites, they went *Down the Strand*, sojourned at the *Old Bull and Bush* or proclaimed to the world in loud voices, while dancing, that *My Girl's a Yorkshire Girl – Yorkshire Through and Through.*

When The Lancers was announced, most of the dancers drew from the floor, leaving it to the experts. The Lancers was traditionally danced with gusto, with loud whoops, exaggerated whirling movements and all the fury of a Cossack sabre dance. The Big Band struck up the opening chords – and away went the dancers on a steady progress towards physical exhaustion. Most of the dancers were middle-aged, some with steel-grey hair at their temples, all with lean frames and with muscles tuned up by much wielding of forks and shifting of milk kits on the farms.

Supper was served. More dancing followed. Progress in a progressive barn dance could be traced by the grunts of the ladies on whose tender feet the less proficient dancers had trodden. Young men discovered, as their right hands were slipped round the waists of new partners for the waltzing sequence, that quite a number of matrons still wore corsets. Yet in the cosy half-light, with the walls patterned by spinning firms and colours emanating from that splendid orb that kept station high above us, like some satellite moon, the cares of the outer world could be forgotten.

Characters Galore

IN HIS PRIME, he stood at over six feet in his stockinged feet and was well-built. Bill Alderson, of Angram, in upper Swaledale, was known as Big Bill in a dale where people had frequently to resort to nicknames to distinguish the members of a few big families. He was also known, like his father, as Bill Up t'Steps. He told me: "If you put on a letter 'Bill, Up t'Steps, Yorkshire, England', it'd just about find me. I've had 'em come like that."

Like many another dalesman in the 1960s, Big Bill, bemused by rapid social changes, was fond of resorting to telling tales of t'auld days. Bill's mother had been a Scott of Swaledale and "her fadder was 96 when he died." Bill grew up with six brothers and sisters on a farm of 80 acres, a mere 18 of them being meadow, in the shadow of the moors on which the family kept a fairly large flock of sheep. Bill was three years old when the 1914-18 war broke out. At the age of five, he was attending Keld School, one and a-half miles away.

He was fond of saying: "At school, we learned more than they do today; we learned a bit o' common sense." Bill was there in wartime, when there were few teachers. "We got t'boss of a woman teacher. If she wanted to keep us in, she couldn't! She once sent us for some sticks she could use if we were naughty; we got her some, but they were rotten."

Forty names were written in the register of that tiny village school. Three Parrington lasses from Tan Hill walked to and from school every day but often stayed in the dale during the week in winter. Children took their mid-day meals to school with them. "Them meals got better at pig-killing time. Then you had sausage and 'crappins'. I've known when children took their tea in tin bottles; a lot of bottles were planted round the stove to warm up."

Dales farmers did not encourage their offspring to waste time. When quite young he took the field paths to Keld, stopping a various barns to fodder the cattle. (Father went the rounds later to "muck out" and "watter t'stock"). Said Bill: "I was nine when I learnt to milk...I started wi' a cow that was fairly quiet. I've never milked with a machine." At haytime, when he was at the tender age of ten, he was mowing with a scythe.

As a schoolboy, he caught rabbits and sold them to make some pocket money. At holiday time in summer, he helped on the grouse moors. And he grew up in a thoroughly Dales household. His father, who did not loiter in bed, started the day off with a bowl of porridge. "Belly keeps t'back up; you can't work wi'out some packing." Mother made butter and cheese. To separate the cream, milk was "set up" in bowls in the cellar. "We used to mark 'em, with a bit o' chalk so we could tell how long they'd stood – for one meal or two meals. The cream was ready when it was hold a penny." On a winter evening, the womenfolk gathered in a room heated by a peat fire and spent hours talking and quilting.

Bill had sharp memories about outdoor life in summer – of days spent at the dusty peat workings from which the dried turves were eventually sledded down to Angram to provide a winter store of fuel. Each fireplace had its "ass-hole," in which the grey powder of incinerated peat accumulated. Such a hole was cleaned out now and again. One man left this operation for so long he backed a horse and cart to the house door and shovelled a mass of ash into the cart.

The sheep could not be left alone for long. Lambing time was arduous for men as well as the sheep. An old-time farmer kept a she-goat which had its kids early. There was a good flow of milk by t'time the sheep were lambing, so if a ewe dried up the lamb could be fed with goats' milk.

When Bill and the young lady who became his wife visited aforementioned Tan Hill inn on a motor bike in the days when the hostelry was run by Susan Peacock, they made a fuss of Susan's few goats, which provided fresh milk for the household and guests. Bill offered one goat an unlighted cigarette, which it "relished." A pipe-smoker standing nearby cut a two-inch long piece from his twist tobacco, which was hard and dark. He offered it to the goat. The twist was eaten. The next jug of milk to appear on the table at Tan Hill would probably have a tobacco flavour.

In winter, hay was taken to the wintering sheep using either a creel, which was a wicker framework a man strapped to his back, or large sacks that dangled on either side of the sure-footed Dales pony that took the shepherd to the moor. Digging out sheep that had been overblown with snow was a weary task. Bill's father used to tell of a sheep that lay in a snowdrift for five days and "came out wick [alive]." That sheep had plenty o' room. "If a sheep gets under a hagg [peat bank] where there's a bit o' room, it can nebble and nebble away. One sheep had 'etten t'wool off another. A sheep'll eat peat if there was nowt else."

Bill helped out during grouse-shooting. He carried guns for an American "till I got fed up. She was bad to deal wi'. Skirts were ower tight and I used to have a job to git her on to t'hoss. Then she had to be loaded up wi' guns and cameras and bags and cigarettes. They were them sweet 'uns. She filled a bag wi' cigarettes every day. To give her credit, she did give a lot of fags to t'lads."

I asked him if he had ever been lost on t'Moors. "I've bin lost – but I've allus fun [found] missen. I kept going till I fun somewhere I knew. At times I've bin a big capped [surprised] where I came out. Someone told me to mak for watter and follow it down. One chap did this for so long he convinced himself that watter was going upbank."

To visit Hawes on Whit Tuesday was a highlight of the year. The Aldersons travelled by horse and trap. It was vital to "hod" the horse near Hawes station, for Swaledale horses were not accustomed to the sound of railway trains nor the clatter of early motor cars. Tot Tommy, a Metcalfe from Keld, ran the Midnight Express over Buttertubs to Hawes. This mini-freight service involved horse and cart. The name was a reference to the slow gait of the horse. "Thoo could hardly tell if he was stopped or going," said Bill. Tommy did keep some unsociable hours; he might set off from Hawes after dark, donning thick clothes, a cap and mittens to protect himself from the wild weather on the Pass.

Another Dales character of the time was Jossie Atkinson, a bachelor farmer. Jossie lived alone at Compstone Hill, one of the string of little farms near the old Roman road between Cotterdale and Hell Gill. He had been at Compstone since 1930 and cheerfully accepted the bad as well as the good days. The farmstead caught the north-westerly gales but the east wind and the notorious Helm Wind "go over the top."

Jossie's father, John, had been a mason as well as a small-time farmer. John had a family of 21 "twice over." One of the family died, so 20 children remained. Then Jossie was born and the figure was back to 21. Everything taken to the farm demanded a special effort. Groceries and loads of coal were delivered to the roadside and moved upbank using a horse and coup, which was a form of sled with a box on it, used main-

ly for carry muck to the pastures. When the "proven man" was a bag short in his delivery, a single bag was left at the roadside and, the horse being out to pasture on the fell, Jossie carried the hundred-weight sack to the farm. He was 70 years old.

Annie Mason, who lived at the head of Wensleydale, had a mind teeming with stories of t'auld days. She was reared at Burtersett. Her father, James Pratt, was an auction-eer, cattle dealer and farmer. She told me of the days when in fine summer weather cows were milked out of doors. "You never bothered to take them into the barn. They either stood in the yard or in a small paddock. It was natural for them to stand and be milked. Cows are creatures of habit. A favourite cow would come and stand against you and rub her head against your shoulders. She knew who you were."

Carrying milk from field to farmhouse was tiring work. "I've carried milk from the low pastures up the hill all the way to Burtersett. I started with a lump on my neck which was tubercular. I was as thin as a lat. My mother sent for the doctor and he turned round to my father and said: 'Jim, you should be ashamed of yourself, allowing your only daughter to do this'. That lump had had been caused by carrying a back-can."

Milk was transported from the farm in 17-gallon kits. "When I was a girl I was not always big enough to reach into the bottom of a can. I remember washing one can when my youngest brother held on to my legs in case I slipped in." Horse and float took some of the milk to the station at Hawes. The first contract was with a dealer in Newcastle; later it went to Burgess of Manchester. "In the dark of winter, trap lambs were used. When I was a small girl, the horse turned so quickly out of the Burtersett road into the main road that I flew off the seat."

And, of course, there is Hannah – indomitable still and, at the time I first knew her, a daleswoman living a solitary life in the old family farm in Baldersdale. She told me: "In summer I live; in winter I exist." She had first come to public attention when a report of a North Pennine organisation mentioned a lady farmer whose income was less than £200 a year. A *Yorkshire Post* reporter visited her and wrote about her simple life. This attracted the attention of a television director. Hannah became a national celebrity. People were fascinated by her struggle for survival and by her simple but firm faith.

In a lyrical period, when Hannah was young and the family complete, there was joy in the annual family jobs, such as haytime, when – with some meadowland and a barn lying about two miles from the farmhouse – the Hauxwells migrated there for a day at a time. Mother packed up the provisions they needed, "including some lovely fried ham." They walked to and from the meadow.

And in the village, small and neat,
I knew each cobble in the street,
And every face that passed me by,
Would have a smile and wink an eye.

                              – When I was young.

P E Copeland.

1970-79

The transformation of the dale-county was well under way, taking the form of "gripping" the moors, ploughing and re-seeding old meadows. In upper Teesdale, water was impounded by giving Cow Green a concrete plug and creating a reservoir in which the ponderous form of Cross Fell, highest point of the Pennines, was reflected. The staff of the Dales National Park was as yet quite small, but visionaries saw a bureaucratic machine in the making.

Oh Deer!

ARTHUR RAISTRICK recalled when the deer park at Bolton in Wharfedale lived up to its name. In earlier times, deer formed a protein bank upon which my lord might draw as a change from the meat that was salted down for winter. The peasantry were left to dream of sinking their teeth into lumps of lean meat.

The ancestors of the deer had ventured into the area some 6,000 years ago when conditions moderated after the million year old spectacular known as the Ice Age. Red deer returned to the Dales when Eric Foster, of Little Newton Farm, near Hellifield railway station, fancied having a few animals to adorn his pastures. They were ordered from a South Country park and arrived – by rail.

As the years went by, and the herd grew in size, this master stockman persuaded the deer to respect the walls. They must leave a pasture via the gate. He would go and talk with them before suggesting a change of grazing. A deer that developed wanderlust gave visitors to the district a surprise. A red stag in the glory of high-spreading antlers was not a common sight in a village transformed by the railway.

A railwayman going off duty startled a stag that had been foraging in a local garden. The panicking deer left a trail of damage as it escaped, leaping from one garden to another. Eric's car was readily identifiable when he was shopping to Settle. You could not help but notice the array of cast antlers on the ledge near the back window of his car.

There was a sense of adventure in visiting the little herd for the approach by car was along a sump-cleaning track from Long Preston. Only once was Eric inhospitable. Word filtered through to me that he had taken exception to a short article I had written about his deer. I turned up unexpectedly. He stood there, his nerves as tense as violin strings, and a torrent of unfriendly words headed my way.

Then Eric stopped talking and said: "You're not shouting back at me." I said, lamely: "It seems I've done something wrong and I'm sorry." The tension between us ended. He slapped me on my back and allowed me to walk out to the deer. A mug of tea was provided in the farmhouse.

Just before I departed, there was the usual prayer meeting. At his command, several dogs leapt on to projecting slates forming a stile on a wall. Another command – and they bowed their heads. Eric said a few words, then delivered a mighty "Amen," at which his dogs leapt down and resumed their normal routine of fratching and dozing.

When, a year or two after Eric's death, the postman reported a mighty deer had turned up at Mike Perrings' farm, west of Giggleswick station, I suspected it was one of Eric's that had escaped the cull.

The deer was sighted in autumn, the time of the red deer rut. Mike allowed me free range on his farm. Half an hour of trudging followed, with no sign of deer. The only unvisited ground was a gill. This was where the big stag had harboured. The Monarch of the Dales lumbered up the side of the gill and stood, majestic, with a backdrop of Ingleborough Hill.

Roe deer, the smallest of the native breeds, returned to the Dales in an enormous pincer-movement. From the southern Lake District came roe of Austrian origin, from a stock introduced to the region near Windermere. They spread into the Lune Valley and crossed into the well-wooded Wenning valley and its tributary gills.

Meanwhile, roe of the old British type that had survived in small numbers on Solway mosses, spread through the new Border conifer forests and worked their way into the northern dales from the east. My first viewing of roe in the upper dales was in the gill behind Matthew Cherry's house at Gunnerside. He reported seeing a deer. A dry cough confirmed it was a buck feeling peevish. Its territory has been violated. Roe are now found wherever there is cover for them. They turned up in the woodland at Malham Tarn House, over 1,000 ft above sea level. One was seen crossing the arid waste of a quarry yard in North Ribblesdale.

My special delight for many years was studying sika deer, of an Asiatic breed introduced to Bowland by Lord Ribblesdale and his pals, to provide sport for the Buckhounds. They were not suited for hunting, having evolved in their native Orient to make a short, sharp dash to cover, where it would remain, still and silent, until danger was past. The Hodgsons of New Ing Farm befriended an orphan sika calf and Arthur Hodgson – with enormous patience – took this hind to the local woods so it might be mated with a wild stag. Hereafter, there was a little herd at New Ing.

On still evenings in autumn I thrilled to the calling of randy sika stags. The sounds were fantastic, being mainly squeals, partly nasal. The silence of a misty evening would be broken as an unseen animal squealed, the call rising and descending, forming a crescent of sound. There followed two or three more squeals. From a distance, they sounded as though they were the merry pipes of Pan

It is said that an arthritic old man was plodding along a farm track when the local sika stag began to call. It was as though someone had suddenly stroked his spine with an icicle. He was so startled, in fact, that he threw away his stick and ran for the first time for years. Like the sika, it was a short dash for cover. It included scrambling over a five-barred gate.

Rural Editor

THE FIRST *Dalesman* editorial office I recall was actually the front room of the double-fronted house that the Scotts were renting from

Ingleborough estate. The walls were lagged with books. Heaps of papers formed highly trippable obstructions on the floor, or what remained of the floor space. There was a daily threat of an avalanche.

A large flat-topped desk, made by a family friend who most certainly did not suffer from agaraphobia occupied eighty per cent of the space. The desk was itself a resting-place for books, for pens, for redundant paper clips and a biro, long expired, and now used for stirring coffee. Harry Scott had used a portable typewriter, now best suited to being displayed in a museum. He preferred to let others do the "tryping,"as he called it.

Harry had the premier position, facing the central part of the desk and with his back to the enclosed stove. Woven into the back of the chair was a piece of stiff paper that could be adjusted to regulate the effect of the stove on the spine. Nearby was the obligatory four-drawer, green filing cabinet, on which repose two wooden trays, holding cards, each bearing the name, address and some factual information of a subscriber to the magazine.

Circulation was built up mainly by sending specimen copies to people in the telephone directory, the presumption at that time being that if anyone had a phone they were moderately wealthy and might afford to subscribe to *The Dalesman*. Harry deduced that five or six people read each copy of the magazine. It would be a boon if a printing ink might be created that would fade a week after the magazine had been opened. Then everyone would have to buy it!

I sat at a corner table, working by the light of a single bulb, with a bent piece of tin as a reflector. Conditions improved a little when we had moved to the new offices, adapted from estate workshops. An early job was filling in a saw-pit. I cannot remember what happened to the estate fire engine, a manual affair, or to the sign BULL AND CAVE, originally intended for a local inn, the property of the estate. The inn had been converted into a farmhouse.

It was in the dining room that the Scotts opened the mail amid a clutter of toast, butter, marmalade, crockery and teapot. The new office, which had a dormer window and a view across the garden to the tower of Clapham church, was soon vacated as the business increased and now I found myself on the ground floor of what had been the Vicar's coachhouse.

The adaptation was carried out by an elderly man wielding a sledge hammer who "brayed" the wall in appropriate places to create windows which were, roughly speaking, where the architect intended them to be. He said he was working by "t'rack o' t'eye." His "fadder" had done so – and what was good enough for his father..." Etc, etc.

Vast quantities of books and papers were stored on the floor above, with results that did not surprise anyone. There were ominous creakings and cracks appeared. The space between floors was a playground and highway for rats that gained access from the remaining part of the long stone and slate building, an area that in its heyday was a barn and was now a cobwebby void.

With a catastrophe in the making, we transferred the heavy stacks of books to the ground floor and the editorial side of *The Dalesman* was elevated. By this time, the magazine had a business manager who meant business. In the old days, what happened was based on how many 10s.6d postal orders (each representing a renewed subscription) came in the post. When four of us took over the running of the company, we kept to the old ways though increased the profit margin. It was not difficult.

I had £50 a month allowed to cover the cost of an issue of the magazine. Hence my meanness when fixing the level of fees paid for contributions. In truth, the level was rigid, with a standard fee of one guinea. Writers and artists had a genuine pleasure in "appearing" in *The Dalesman*. A wealthy businessman who contributed paintings in the form of sets of printing blocks, each set valued at over £100 (a fortune to us), had his work used because it provided colour cheaply. One picture was entitled River Aire at Cottingley. It was modernist in the sense of being, er – a daub. A local reader sent me a postcard:

Aire river? Nay, nivver!
But it maks no matter
Cos I can't see t'watter.

There was joy in a country editorship. In spring, curlews glided overhead, bubbling over with song. For a while, there was the cheery whistle of Dick Clarke, ex-signalman, as he went on his rounds with coffee and biscuits. Dick had a complexion like a turkey cock because his wife Sally insisted he wore flannel shirts the year through. He would arrive, panting. Tea had usually slopped into the saucer. He rummaged in the pockets of his blue serge trousers and then triumphantly brought out – a chocolate biscuit.

I made a special point of going out on one day of the week, to keep my finger on the pulse of Yorkshire/Lakeland life. Sometimes, when I left the office, I had no certain idea where I would go and what I would do. At the T-junction, at the main road, I could either turn left for Yorkshire or right for the Lakes. Once, I gave the car its head, turning as the mood took me, stopping only when I reached the end of a cul de sac, which was at the remote hamlet of Stean, in the upper valley of the Nidd. The natives were friendly!

In the office, there was a continuous flurry of paper as articles were written on a rickety typewriter and the many contributions were subedited. Virtually every article could be improved by deleting the first paragraph. The liveliest items were letters from readers. I tended to accept more than I could reasonably use, not wishing to turn down any good *Dalesman* material. Material was returned with a personal letter. I was often tempted to use the Chinese form of rejection, which was: "Your honourable contribution is too good for our pages."

Below Ground

How diverse man's choice in pleasure
As applied to hours of leisure!
There are those who only treasure
Seaside joys as ones of worth;
Some are all for mountaineering,
Others find the plains more cheering,
While some plump for disappearing
In the bowels of the earth.

SO WROTE a newspaper poet about those whose pleasure was found in exploring the caves and potholes of the dale-country. Their headlamps lit up a world of shafts and galleries eroded along fault lines in the limestone by water which had picked up a weak solution of acid from the air and vegetation. It was a world that evolved in darkness and was adorned by calcite formations, such as stalactites (they hang on tight) and stalagmites (which grow from the floor) and pillars (which occur where the two join).

Local people tended to shake their heads sadly at those whose pleasure consisted of being squashed and muddied far from daylight. One old lady said to a young man who was carrying a rope ladder: "Are you one of these pothoiler chaps?" He nodded. She looked at him pityingly and said: "Doesn't ta think tha'll spend enuff time below t'ground without going there now?"

In the late 19th century, the Yorkshire Ramblers went to earth in style. A club that included influential members of the middle-class talked to Dales landowners on equal terms and during a Meet were untroubled by others. One or two members had their own rope ladders to enable them to emulate Orpheus and go to the underworld, with provisions that included smoked salmon, beef sandwiches and half chickens, also the odd bottle of wine. Percy Robinson, when catering at the Gaping Gill Meet, usually contrived to provide cutlery and serviettes.

The first potholers I knew wore their oldest clothes and large hats packed with straw. They had studded boots and descended rifts in the limestone using unwieldy ladders of hemp, with wooden rungs. Soon, overalls and a metal helmet were the acceptable wear. Blackburn Holden, a textile man, chose cotton ropes for the ladders with which he descended the 340 ft of the main shaft of GG. He had not reckoned with the elasticity of cotton and, when he wished to return, had trod on some 20 rungs before that elasticity was taken up and he was actually rising. It was Bottrill who had a technological breakthrough. Noticing that a potholer only had one foot on one rung at one time, he made his ladders half the normal width, saving weight and space.

A photographer who wished to capture the immense size of the main chamber of GG – a chamber having all the majesty of a cathedral – set up his plate camera on a tripod, left the shutter cap off for a long expo-

sure and "lit" the chamber using screwed up newspaper and flash-powder. He scuttered about the floor of GG igniting the paper. Clouds of smoke followed the flashes. The photographer then had the daunting task of re-locating his camera so that he might replace the lens cap.

Reg Hainsworth, doyen of Yorkshire potholers, and now well into his nineties, "shot" a pioneering underground film, relating to the rescue of a dog from the Alum Pot system. Painstakingly, he and his friends lugged wet batteries into the system to provide light for filming. One day, as they were about to "shoot", someone released flash powder from far down Alum Pot and filled the air with smoke.

Journals produced by the clubs in the inter-war years had amusing passages, such as when a potholer was see jog-trotting through a chamber "with a boulder half the size of Leeds Town Hall trundling slowly behind him." In *Caves and Caving* the speleologist was defined as "one of the (fortunately) lesser known mammals. They shun the daylight and, although only partly nocturnal, spend many daylight hours in holes in the earth. Although gifted with legs they prefer to crawl on their stomachs. Such are their dirty habits that they are happier lying in the mud than on dry ground. When met in the dark they resemble huge glow-worms and, although scientists cannot find a reason, the light is at the other end!"

For those who could not face the prospect of clambering into the underworld on a swaying rope ladder, there was the pleasure of sauntering into a show cave, as Ingleborough Cave, near Clapham, where the old-time guides were inclined to lay on some entertainment. Harry Harrison, grandson of Josiah, who was among those who opened up the system by breaking through a stalagmitic barrier in 1837, fancied himself as a poet. When he had a captive audience, at the far end of the cave, he would read examples of his verse and even offer some printed examples for sale.

Here is part of Harry Harrison's account of how his grandfather had "opened Nature's doors" at Ingleborough Cave:

> *He persevered to cut four-feet thick wall*
> *Nor heeded danger from a pent-up flood;*
> *As just with pick-axe force behind he stood,*
> *An unknown task, truly explorer's role.*

Dalesfolk took a little while to become
accustomed to t'wireless, which broke down
their age-old isolation …

1980-89

Rural post offices, village shops and schools, were closing at a worrying rate. As a schoolgirl wrote: "If there were many more few of them, there wouldn't be enough!" Bolton Hall estate in Wensleydale entered the high-tech age by acquiring a 350-cow dairy unit, incorporating a herringbone milking parlour. Five bunk-barns were opened in the Dales National Park. They provided basic overnight self-catering accommodation for visitors. One barn was situated at remote Cam Houses, where ramblers cross the watershed twixt the Wharfe and the Ribble.

Show Business

I GAVE a retired Craven farmer a lift by car to Gargrave Show. Impressed by the large attendance, I asked him to estimate the number of people in the field. "Nay," he protested. I persisted, having admired the way a Dales farmer counts a flock of scurrying sheep. He said: "If you can get those folk to run through yon gateway, I'll soon tell you."

Showtime is a good time to see the flighty hill sheep at close quarters. Animals that in the great outdoors run off at your approach are now in a confined space. There have been times when I have given a rigged or kisted sheep a helping hand. Then, having turned on its back, it is incapable of turning back. If you see a rigged sheep, upskuttle it. Better still, get the farmer to do it, to avoid injury.

In a show situation, all a proud Swaledale tup can do is butt you – or peevishly butt the fence. These hill sheep are relatively small, with hard, tight fleeces that don't drag at snowtime. It's a wonder sheep don't suffer from mange, judging by the number of times a year they are handled. It happens for tupping, dipping, lambing, spaining [separation of yows from lambs] and clipping.

When the Dales show season arrives, the very best sheep are on view. I overheard a farmer say: "Yon tup has a pedigree." His neighbour, who wanted to buy it cheap, replied: "Well – I've nivver sin a sheep more in need o' yan [one]."

There's no business like show business, especially in Swaledale, where shows at Tan Hill, Muker and Reeth have kept a thoroughly local flavour. The same also applies to Malhamdale and the sports at Leyburn and a handful of other shows that are highlights in the social year as well as a testing time for livestock.

Kilnsey has a huge show, held in the shadow of the famous Crag. The dales flavour is here and at the annual dinner, which I once had the honour to address. I re-cycled the best Dales stories but it was the chairman who "topped t'stack" with a tale about an old lady in a nursing home. As she and a friend sat in the lounge, she remarked: "I'm bored stiff. I think I'll take all my clothes off and streak through the place."

Her friend was appalled, but the lady was as good as her word. She stripped off and made her best possible speed through the lounge. As she passed two poor-sighted old men who were sitting just inside the door, one said: "Was that Edna?" The other replied: "I think so." Said the first old chap: "By gum, but she want's her dress ironing."

It was at Pateley Bridge show, the last in the season, that I heard of the stingy old couple who, late in life, invested in an old tractor, of which they were inordinately proud. When the old man died, his widow went to the office of the local newspaper to insert a death notice in the next issue. When the cost was mentioned, she was appalled. The young lady behind the counter said: "This week we have a special offer – the first five words for nothing." The widow brightened and said: "Put down: 'Jack died. Tractor for sale'."

At Muker, where gossip – the small-change of Dales life – abounds, I first watched the champion band muster outside the pub, play some popular music, then – headed by show officials – march to the showground. The steward at the gate collected my £1, stamped my hand with the word "Muker" and smiled as a sheep farmer said to me: "Thoo wants to be thankful he didn't clip a bit out of an ear." That had been the procedure for a thousand years and more – since Norse times, when a law-mark became a "lug" mark. Not so long ago, an unruly child had his "lug clattered."

Judging the sheep proceeded along traditional lines. The judges were not over-awed by the presence of some of the keenest flockmasters in the Dales. It was important to prolong the judging, to give the impression of careful thought and also, as in all good shows, to keep people in suspense. The judges took in the general characteristics of the sheep. They then parted the wool, testing its quality, looking for "black bits." Ewes suffered a loss of dignity when they were turned on to their backs, then reared in a sitting position, where their bellies sagged. The tits were carefully examined. As one judge told me later: "Some tits can be duds."

Among the competitions at Muker Show was welly-throwing. "Screwed up" wellies were pronounced out of order, though no one objected when a competitor spent ten minutes ramming the sides of wellies into the feet to lesson the wind resistance as it flew through the air. In the village hall, trestle tables had been joined together and covered with food – beef and ham, lettuce and pickles, trifle and cream, meringue, apple pie and cream cakes. Coffee was available. The diners had a choice of port or sherry.

At the pens, in the relative quiet of the afternoon, the farmers continued to discuss the fine points about sheep. A latecomer arrived. "Hoo is ta?" said one man. "All reet. Taties oot. Cows laid in." The supreme champion tup was one bought at the autumn sales, where the proud owner had paid £16,000 for it. It was said to be "a good doer."

If I'd paid sixteen thousand pounds for a sheep, I'd be worried every time it coughed.

Fairest Amerdale

ARNCLIFFE, in the "deep fork of Amerdale" – as Wordsworth wrote of Littondale – was the first of the Dales villages to experi-

123

ence being the setting for a television series, being the backdrop for *Emmerdale Farm*. For four years, vehicles bearing equipment, film crew and performers trundled up from the Leeds studios of Yorkshire Television for sequences that needed a true Dales setting.

The old church by the Skirfare was the venue for spoof weddings and funeral services. It was said that a local farmer, returning home from Skipton one Market Monday, felt queezy when he saw a hearse. Who had died? It turned out to be just another dramatic episode in the Emmerdale saga. Another day, in a period of drought, a red fire engine arrived, drew water from the river and pumped it over the roof of a moorside barn to simulate heavy rain.

The television company's "secret" location soon became known to the fans. Then a Yorkshire journalist mentioned the village by name. Soon, hundreds of gawpers were watching their favourite "soap" being filmed. *Emmerdale Farm* was moved to a "secret" location nearer Leeds.

Arncliffe soon shrugged off this loss of modern glamour. Arncliffe has a grand setting, with limestone scars and a river that flows as clear and cool as when Charles Kingsley's water-babies gavorted here. Mellow buildings stand around a green in neat formation, as though on parade. The church, a little off-centre, is partly screened by ancient yews in a churchyard that each spring has drifts of snowdrops and aconites.

The Falcon, formerly *The Leg of Mutton*, is still run by the Miller family, who maintain a tradition of inn-keeping and farming that began in the 1860s. It was then that James Miller, who had been keeping the *Drover's Arms* on Dallowgill Moor, became a tenant of the Hammond family when he moved to the inn at Arncliffe. M'duke Miller, a local Poo-bah in the sense that he kept himself busy with a variety of jobs, was famous locally as an artist. His water-colours are still greatly prized. His son, David, keeps to the traditional ways and recalls an Easter Week-end when his patrons established a local record by consuming 20 barrels of beer.

At Arncliffe I was reminded of some of the folk who traded with the locals, including Newland Dean, a butcher with a large round, who habitually set off from Grassington in an old Austin van about teatime, playing the odd game of dominoes in his round of the farms. He arrived at Arncliffe so late that he was nicknamed The Midnight Butcher. He returned home in the early hours. Mr Denny was a maker of oatcake. Whistling Jimmy came with haberdashery, carrying four large packs, in one which were sweets for the children.

The Middletons told me of a venerable billy goat that had occupied territory between Kilnsey Crag and Blue Scar. The goat had died some 12 years before. When it was decided to hold a fancy dress dance, a local man made himself a "cave man" outfit and expressed a wish to take t'auld billy goat with him to the dance. The gamekeeper and a friend went to the fell to catch the ancient warrior. They eventually cornered him on a ledge and lassooed him.

The goat was kept in a croft for two days before the dance took place. Two village children who showed interest in the goat were offered half a crown each if they could ride him. They managed it with some effort, though their parents immediately regretted it when they detected a pungent goaty smell on their clothes. Male goats have such a nasty pong in autumn they customarily walk into the wind so that they do not have to breathe in their own smell. That, at least, was suggested to me at Arncliffe, where the reluctant billy goat was dragged to the dance by the "cave man."

When everyone complained of the smell, and the goat was released, it dashed into the darkness. Next day, the animal was back on Blue Scar.

Radio Times

TELEVISION was regarded warily by dalesfolk when it was introduced and villagers gathered around a few sets with 12" screens to watch pictures that were transmitted in scintillating black-and-white. A couple from a remote farm who visited Skipton looked into a shop window where a Bendix washing machine was being demonstrated. The man watched the swirling images for a moment or two, then said: "I don't reckon much to television."

Dalesfolk took a little while to become accustomed to t'wireless, which broke down their age-old isolation by putting them in regular touch with the outside world. A sense of wonder at how it worked remained and when it was suggested to a Wensleydale grand-dad that he might get another set, he retorted: "I'se just getten used to t'folk on this one."

The best of t'wireless was in the 1930s, when folk tuned in to Romany, the Methodist minister with a gipsy background whose weekly jaunts held listeners to *Children's Hour* enthralled. It was a shock to them when they discovered the "walks" took place in the studio, with rural sounds simulated and introduced by an back-up team. Coconut shells and a sandpit gave a fair representation of a horse's hooves.

Bertha Lonsdale, a West Riding librarian, contributed to *Children's Hour* some arresting material, ranging from railway history to regional celebrities like Lady Anne Clifford and her five castles in the Craven and Westmorland Dales. Bertha worked at a time when a mobile broadcasting unit consisted of a large seven-seater saloon car from which the two extra seats had been removed to hold batteries and the disc-cutting gear. In this pre-tape age, discs were the equivalent of gramophone records. The recording car was parked as near as possible to the site of the recording, the maximum distance being that of two fifty foot cables joined together.

Taken one day to see Belah railway viaduct, in the northern dale country, Bertha viewed the wide, austere landscape and said to a railway linesman who was standing nearby: "What a gorgeous view you've got." He replied: "Aye, miss, but it's about all we've getten."

In 1936, the BBC recording van poked its bonnet into remote Gunnerside and collected material for a schools programme. It was a year after a radio character called Harry Hopeful discovered the waspish Susan Peacock at Tan Hill Inn. The BBC kept its finger on the pulse of local life and introduced to the world songs like *Beautiful Swaledale*, composed by one of the Reynoldson family. Over the air waves came the *Swaledale Dirge*, a chant sung by mourners as they plodded along the Corpse Road towards Grinton Kirk.

In the golden age of radio, people dressed up and listened in silence to favourite programmes like *Saturday Night Theatre*. Ere long, the older folk would stay at home and the youngsters depart in their cars for – who knaws where? In 1958, the BBC broadcast from within Alum Pot. Aerials were erected on the moor and the broadcast received at Selside, in the valley, from where it would be transmitted by land line.

Television came to the North in October, 1952, with the opening of the Holme Moss transmitter, bleakly situated on a Pennine ridge over 1,700 ft above sea level. I remember standing on the moor, looking at the base of the lofty mast, a rigid structure held by guy ropes and reposing on a single ball bearing that would permit it to move rather than snap in extreme weather conditions. The clerk of works told me that snow had lain on the ground for six of the nineteen months it was under construction.

The 1980s flooded the Dales with sound and vision. A modern Tower of Babel was created. Most of the comedy was now, to quote a daleswoman, "too daft to laugh at" and sex and violence were beginning to rear their ugly heads.

Moving pictures of any sort have had their day. I have far more demand for slide shows than movies.

Richard Kearton, an early populariser of natural history through photography, writing in February, 1925.

1990-99

Dales farmers are becoming demoralised by a downturn in their conditions. The Dales – once so quiet – are now vibrant with traffic, both on the roads and in the air, which shivers to the passage of low-flying military aircraft. People visiting a Dales museum see models of farmers and plastic cows. Now that sheep prices are low and lambs are worth next-to-nothing, some farmers are keeping ostriches, red deer, even water buffaloes. And, as mentioned, members of the Rylstone Women's Institute have posed in large hats – in only large hats – for a calendar sponsored by a brewery. What would the prim old-time Dales Methodists have said about that?

A Day at the Palace

"ANYTHING in the post?" I asked. "Nothing much," said Freda. "Just another letter from the Inland Revenue." It was not the usual buff colour though it did hint at officialdom. Printed along the top were the words: "On Her Majesty's Service." The envelope lay unopened for several hours. Then I glanced at it again. At the bottom, left, were the words "Prime Minister." I gulped, stood to attention, saluted and opened the envelope.

The Prime Minister must have been busy that day for the letter came from "your obedient servant," Alex Allan. Further scrutiny revealed that he was not so much my servant as the Prime Minister's – his Principal Private Secretary, indeed. He wrote: "The Prime Minister has asked me to inform you, in strict confidence...he has it in mind...submit my name to the Queen...Birthday Honours...you be appointed a Member of the Order of the British Empire."

My eyes leapt along the lines. Then I sat down and said: "Whew!" Freda said: "This means I'll have to buy a new hat." The Citation (to be printed in the *London Gazette*) was "for services to Journalism and to the community in Yorkshire and Cumbria." It was the Year of the Honours. Eight long years after I (theoretically) retired from journalism, the Yorkshire Dales Society bestowed on me an honorary membership. The University of Bradford had given me the honorary degree of Doctor of Letters, prompting our postman to say: "What time's t'surgery oppen?" One of the Bradford academics remarked: "What does it feel like to have been doctored?"

The date for the London investiture was fixed for November 21. Freda, daughter Janet and I travelled by train to London. At King's Cross, the sun was shining, the station was immaculate and the city folk we met were affable. There was hope for the city!

Janet took over the organisation. We went by Underground to our Hyde Park Gate hotel. Janet rang up our son David, using the number of his mobile phone. She asked him where he was. He replied: "On the train, near Wigan..." In London, he used a taxi, which was just as well. There had been a power failure. The whole of the Underground had stopped. Thousands of people were temporarily trapped.

November 21 began not so much with a fanfare as with the clatter of dustbins from the street. We dressed languidly. A taxi had been arranged for 9-40 a.m. It was a Mercedes, driven by a pleasant, soft-spoken Pakistani who, with time in hand, drove through some of the city's most elegant streets – rows of huge terraced houses, uniformly white, contrasting with the desert-brown of the domed Harrods. Our driver's family had emigrated from Pakistan to Bradford to work in the mills. The son moved to London and acquired a share in a taxi firm that just about broke even in winter but thankfully made a profit from the tourists in summer.

Outside Buckingham Palace, we had our photograph taken by a Bradfordian, "the last of the Listers who had the mill." He charged £30 and said he would post on the prints. We did not doubt him. A few wide-eyed tourists were watching a procession of posh cars being driven into the Palace Yard, where Guardsmen stood as stiff and silent as herons. We progressed to the inner courtyard and to a grand sorting out – a separation of the participants and their guests.

Our surroundings were spectacular. The décor was white and gold, as it had been since Edward VII had changed the previously drab colour scheme. The grand staircase was, er – grand. The toilets were plush. Guardsmen in full dress had be-plumed helmets, mirror-bright breastplates and gleaming swords. I left my top hat at the cloakroom and was ushered along a passage and into a room that was high, ornate, adorned with paintings made familiar by their use in books. We were told the investiture would be by the Prince of Wales. A rumour that the Queen was in bed was not correct. She was in Bedford.

A metal clip was attached to my jacket. My medal would be slipped over it. Small groups of us walked in line ahead along galleries festooned with paintings. Then, through an open door, I had my first view of the magnificence of the ballroom and the balcony on which a group of military musicians was playing familiar strains – *Blaze Away, Barcarolle* and Novello's *Leap Year Waltz.*

I had to walk (on a red carpet) to an usher and wait here until my name was called. The citation was read out. Walking a few more paces, I turned left, gave a short bow and advanced towards the Prince of Wales, mindful of what one of the officials had said: "Go fairly close, so he will not have to reach out too far, and on no account join him on the dais." Here was a Prince who was not unfamiliar with the Dales. He had lodged here for short periods at the home of an old friend. He had painted the Dales landscape, coping well with its transient weather system.

The Prince, who was now in naval uniform, had a slight stoop and a bald patch on the back of his head. (That made at least two of us). He inquired about the outlets for my writing. He then smiled, offered a firm handclasp (a signal that this mini-audience was over). I walked back-wards a yard or two, bowed again, turned right and strode out of the Ballroom, where I was de-clipped and the medal, the MBE, handed to me in a special case.

When it was all over, and the National Anthem had been played for the second time; the Prince departed with his colourful escort of Yeomen. The company slowly dispersed through the Ballroom, down the Grand Staircase, between the impassive figures of Guardsmen and into the hard autumn sunlight.

Jam and Jerusalem

FIFTY YEARS ago, when I first addressed a Women's Institute meet-ing up t'Dales, I was a solitary man, sitting at the back of a group representing almost every woman in the district. The chairman – as she was still known – was clad in the obligatory tweeds, twin-set and pearls. It was summer. The members wore their print dresses and home-knitted cardigans almost as a uniform.

There were minor humiliations, such as when the lady who normal-ly presided was on holiday and she who deputed to lead the meeting said: "Mrs Smith is in Majorca. How we all wish we were with her." As impending speaker, I had a sudden uprush of capillary action on my face. Harry Scott told the story of the chairperson who reminded the members that she had been asked to find a celebrated wit. "I couldn't find a wit, so I've brought two half-wits."

I was occasionally provided with overnight accommodation when visiting distant Institutes. Once, it was in a castle. I was ushered into a room with a four-poster bed. Next morning, in the breakfast room, I was asked if I had seen the ghost. "Ghost?" "Oh, Katherine Parr walks now and again."

Every meeting opened with *Jerusalem*. Everyone stood. The business meeting began. At this stage, the invited speaker – realising there was much business, including several long-winded reports, stifled a yawn. It amazed me how much paperwork accumulated from month to month. Once, the business part of the meeting was so protracted, I was told my time for talking had shrunk to a quarter of an hour.

At that meeting, an equally bored member told me the story of the husband of a Women's Institite member who, reading his library book, turned a page to find a note from his wife: "When you've got to here, take the pie out of the oven." And I was told about a man who persuaded a neighbour to help him drive a pig into the house. He then requested his help to man-handle the pig up the steps and place it in the bath.

When asked why he needed to do this, he blamed his wife, who whenever he returned home with an item of gossip simply said: "I know." She was now at a Women's Institute meeting. He would be in bed when she returned late. Her first task was to go to the bathroom. That night she would rush into the bedroom, wake him up and say: "There's a pig in the bath!" And he would simply remark: "I know."

I was not to know, in the halcyon days of long ago that an organisation I had thought of as being prim, even prudish, would suddenly capture the attention of the world through the activity of a dozen members in a small Dales community. In a region where, at the beginning of the 20th century, some prim folk covered up the legs of the table on Sundays, the average WI calendar featured "village greens, hills, dales and postboxes," to quote one of the members.

The ladies at Rylstone decided to take everything off for a series of photographs to be used on a calendar marking a new Millennium. Any profits would go to the Leukaemia Research Fund, in memory of a well-regarded local man who developed the disease. Individuals posed to represent the months of the year. Such "props" as broad-brimmed hats and strings of pearls would tastefully obscure "hairy parts and bottoms."

The calendar would be prepared in such great secrecy that not even the husbands of the "models" would know about it until it was officially launched. The ladies even toyed with the idea of heading for the woods dressed in bin liners that would be removed for a short time for the pictures. "But by this time it had got to October and we thought it would be a bit cold." In the end, they were "shot" at the home of one of the members by her photographer-artist husband, a guarantee it would be artistic.

Said one of the members: "While it's a far cry from jam and Jerusalem, the result is a tasteful yet revealing calendar of which we are all very proud." What would the leukaemia sufferer have thought of the idea? He apparently knew about it before he died. The idea of getting this group of spirited daleswomen to make a saucy departure from Jam and Jerusalem to pose for a calendar kept him laughing to the end.

A Women's Institute spokesman in London described the group's actions as a "one off." All, 3,000 copies of the revealing calendar, sold out in barely a day and a further large print run was ordered.

Highspot of the Dales

I HAVE just climbed Whernside – I think! Wind, rain and thick mist – a common Pennine "mix" – combined to produce conditions that lay somewhere between atrocious and diabolical. Whernside is the "attic" of the Yorkshire Dales National Park. Its whale-like form provides a backdrop to Ribblehead Viaduct.

Whernside is less shapely than its near-neighbours, Ingleborough and Penyghent, yet those who stand at the highest point, 2,419ft, in clear weather have the dale-country at their feet. When I arrived at the usual parking ground near the T-junction at Ribblehead, there was not another car in sight. Somewhere out in the cloying greyness lurked a 24-arch railway viaduct with a maximum height of just over 100 ft. On that day, fifty thousand cubic yards of masonry had vanished.

I plodded towards where I thought the viaduct might be and eventually it materialised in the mist. My route had led directly to Pier 13. I shivered. The wind played an oboe solo between the arches. I was reminded of an old story – that a railwayman crossing the viaduct had his cap lifted from his head by a gale. The cap was blown under an arch, up the other side and fell on his head. It was not a perfect landing. The neb of the cap was facing backwards. Such a story is unlikely. A westering wind is deflected upwards by the parapets.

Two yellow dumper trucks, with scoops full of "quarry bottoms," lumbered by, churning up yellow mud in the puddles. They made a grand exit, somewhere beyond the viaduct. I intended to take the high road to Blea Moor signal; box, thence to the newly-restored aqueduct just south of Blea Moor Tunnel and the footpath by Force Gill to the flanks of Whernside. When I re-established contact with the drivers of the dumper trucks, they were depositing the quarry bottoms on the path.

After waving at the Blea Moor signalman – his box was like an outpost in a desert – I found myself in an area where chuckling becks had become raging, peat-brown torrents. When the Settle-Carlisle railway was under construction in the 1870s, and the weather was at its Pennine worst, conditions were so bad at Ribblehead that a light cart with a barrel rather than wheels was used to transport equipment over boggy ground. No one gave much thought to the poor horse that must haul the cart.

In due course, and with sodden feet, I reached the aqueduct and had my first glimpse of Force Gill, a route up Whernside favoured by Mr Wainwright; it is not on the official path. The steep-sided valley was a turmoil of thundering water and spray. The main waterfall, second cousin to Hardraw and Thornton Force, had been transformed by heavy rain into a Yorkshire Niagara.

I plodded on. The incessant rain beat a tattoo against the hood of my anorak. With increasing elevation, the wind was stronger. I climbed in a dull, grey world, with visibility limited to a few yards. Thankfully, the footpath had been reinforced with stone slabs. My route was clear to see. Using that path was a strange experience, for on to it was pouring surface water from the ground on either side. A shallow, pulsing flow covered the big flat stones. It was like walking on a beck-bottom.

At the summit of Whernside, I sought the lee of the drystone wall, where someone had raised a plank on stones, providing a handy seat. A Swaledale sheep wandered into view, realised there were no scraps of food to be had and went sorrowfully away. The glorious view of Ingleborough from Whernside had been blotted out by mist.

Normally, I would have returned to my car by the same route but the wind was chill and, to quote the Good Book, "the day was far spent." I took the direct descent to the Nordic farmsteads at the foot of the mountain. Whernside sheltered me from the worst of the wind. My path lay through local meadows. I had a tantalising glimpse through an uncurtained window of a living room with roaring fire and mellow lighting.

I freed a lamb that had been trapped by the neck in wire netting. It was almost dark as I walked beside a foaming beck near Winterscales, passed under the immense arches of Ribblehead viaduct and crossed the moor. Since my walk began, the local becks had risen. There was water, water everywhere. I climbed thankfully into the car, where I was sheltered from the fury of wind and rain. Now there were two thoughts in mind – the prospect of hot soup and a hot bath.